Praise for William Ury and *Getting Past No*

"William Ury is an acknowledged authority on negotiating in difficult situations, and this book leaves no doubt as to the reason."
—John Kenneth Galbraith

"As the world changes, negotiation is becoming the primary form of decision-making, and this is the best book on the subject. It's worth its weight in gold."
—John Naisbitt and Patricia Aburdene, co-authors of *Megatrends 2000*

"*Getting Past No* is the most elegant handbook on the challenge of difficult negotiation and difficult people. No negotiation will ever be too tough again."
—Leonard A. Lauder, president, Estée Lauder Companies

"Bill Ury has a remarkable ability to get to the heart of a dispute and find simple but innovative ways to resolve it."
—President Jimmy Carter

Getting Past No was awarded the Book Prize of the Center for Public Resources "for excellence and innovation."

GETTING PAST NO

Negotiating in Difficult Situations

Revised Edition

WILLIAM URY

BANTAM BOOKS
New York Toronto London Sydney Auckland

GETTING PAST NO
A Bantam Book

PUBLISHING HISTORY
Bantam hardcover edition published September 1991
Bantam trade paperback edition / February 1993
Bantam trade paperback reissue / March 2007

Published by
Bantam Dell
A Division of Random House, Inc.
New York, New York

Cover design by Tom McKeveny

Library of Congress Catalog Card Number: 91-10101

ISBN 978-0-553-37131-4

Printed in the United States of America
Published simultaneously in Canada

www.bantamdell.com

RRC 40 39 38 37 36 35 34 33

*For Roger Fisher
with gratitude*

CONTENTS

Author's Note, Fifteen Years Later

It has now been fifteen years since the publication of *Getting Past No*. Although the world has changed a good deal, the principles and methods presented here for dealing with difficult people and difficult situations remain as timely and needed as ever.

The importance and pervasiveness of negotiation have only continued to grow. A generation or so ago, it is fair to say that most decisions were made hierarchically. The people on the top gave the orders and the people on the bottom simply followed them. That is changing. Nowadays, in every domain, from family to work to politics, negotiation is becoming the preeminent form of making decisions. This is a global phenomenon I think of as the Negotiation Revolution.

But it is not easy to negotiate. If anything, there are more difficulties, disputes, and conflicts than ever in today's networked world. Conflict is a growth industry—and so, naturally, are difficult negotiations. It is perhaps not surprising that the interest in the negotiating methods described here in *Getting Past No* has continued to grow.

I have often been asked how my thinking about negotiation has evolved in the time since I wrote *Getting Past No*. Although I would change little or nothing in this book, which has stood the test of time, I have just written a new book about negotiation—curiously enough, about how to *say* No—in a positive and constructive fashion. It may be useful therefore to say a word about the relationship, as I have come to understand it, among the three books I have written and co-written about negotiation, beginning with *Getting to Yes.*

Getting to Yes marks its twenty-fifth anniversary this month. Roger Fisher and I wrote it to address the challenge of adversarial conflict and the increasing need for cooperative negotiation at home, at work, and in the larger world. It continues to be found useful by a large readership around the world.

Ten years after the publication of *Getting to Yes*, I wrote *Getting Past No* in response to perhaps the most common question posed by readers of the first book: "Sure, I'd like to get to Yes, but what if the other side's answer is No? What if they don't *want* to cooperate?" People want to know how to bring about cooperation and sustain it in the face of the seemingly insuperable obstacles we all face every day: attacks and counterattacks, anger and suspicion, ingrained habits of hard bargaining, interests that appear irreconcilable, and efforts to win through intimidation and power plays.

Getting Past No distills what I have learned over many years from my own experiences as a negotiator and mediator in a wide range of business, political, and interpersonal situations as well as from the systematic observation of successful negotiators in these different arenas. There are a multitude of useful techniques, but many of us find it hard to remember them in the midst of a heated negotiation. Therefore, I have tried in this book to organize what works into an all-purpose, five-step strategy called Breakthrough Negotiation. It represents my best answer to the question of how to win the cooperation of others in a world of strongly felt differences.

My latest book is *The Power of a Positive No*, subtitled

How to Say No and Still Get to Yes. I have written it in response to another "growth industry"—the astronomical increase in the demands being made on each of us in this era of overload and overwork, ever-expanding e-mail, and eroding ethics.

Though one might at first think that I'm working at cross purposes if I'm teaching both how to say No and how to get past No, the truth is that the principles in *The Power of a Positive No* and *Getting Past No* are congruent and mutually reinforcing. They are also consistent with the principles in *Getting to Yes*.

Getting to Yes maps out the way to Yes, a mutually satisfactory agreement. *Getting Past No*—this book—shows how to navigate the obstacles that stand betweeen you and Yes. For each of us encounters difficult people and difficult situations every day. *The Power of a Positive No* describes how to say No when it is vital to stand up and protect your core interests and values. It is not just about how to say No, however, but about how to do so in a respectful and constructive manner that can potentially lead to agreement. As its subtitle indicates, it is about how to say No and *still* get to Yes.

Ultimately, all of my books are about getting to Yes. Every one of us, many times a day, finds ourselves in the dance of negotiation, the dance of Yes and No. Sometimes we are in the role of the person saying No, and sometimes we are in the role of the person trying to get past No. Just as a great dance calls on both dancers to do their best, just as great sports games happen only when both teams play their best, so it is with negotiation. You get to the most satisfying solutions and the most optimal relationships when both sides are doing their best to engage the very real problems dividing them.

So, while each of the three books can stand alone, they

are deeply complementary. I have come to see all three as a trilogy about the life skills necessary for successful negotiation. If each of us goes into negotiations with a good faith effort to get to Yes, and each of us learns how to say No when necessary and how to get past No when possible, our lives will be happier and more prosperous, and the world will be a better place.

Let me end by saying that it has been my pleasure to have used the simple five-step method described in *Getting Past No* and to have witnessed thousands of other people using it effectively for many years now. I wish you, the reader, much success in your own negotiations to come. May this method for getting past No truly serve you, those around you, and our larger world!

William Ury
Boulder, Colorado
September 2006

Acknowledgments

In working on successive drafts of this book, I often felt like the opera tenor whose finale was greeted with enthusiastic cries of "Encore! Encore!" After the fifth encore, the tenor asked the audience, "How many more times do you want me to sing?" And the answer came back: "Until you get it right!"

My audience has been equally demanding. I am immensely grateful for the comments and suggestions of those who read drafts, including Linda Antone, James Botkin, William Breslin, Nancy Buck, Stephen Goldberg, Richard Haass, Deborah Kolb, Linda Lane, David Lax, Martin Linsky, David Mitchell, Bruce Patton, John Pfeiffer, John Richardson, Carol Rinzler, Jeffrey Rubin, James Sebenius, Dayle Spencer, William Spencer, Daniel Stern, Douglas Stone, Elizabeth Ury, and Janice Ury.

I should also mention my enormous debt to the Program on Negotiation at Harvard Law School. Over more than a decade my colleagues there have provided me with intellectual stimulation and camaraderie. My ideas on negotiation have been forged and tested in the freewheeling seminars and conversations that take place under the Program's hospitable roof.

My colleague Roger Fisher introduced me to the field of negotiation over fifteen years ago and generously served as a mentor. Together we coauthored two books, the second being *Getting to Yes*. My debt to Roger is so great it can be properly acknowledged only on the dedication page.

Another Harvard colleague and friend, Ronald Heifetz, generously allowed me to use his evocative phrase "going to the balcony," a metaphor for taking a step back and getting some perspective.

I would also like to thank two able research assistants. Sarah Jefferys and Annette Sassi rummaged through the Harvard libraries for relevant books and articles, assiduously collecting negotiation examples. In addition, Annette wrote many insightful memos commenting on the evolving manuscript.

Throughout the process my assistant Sheryl Gamble proved indefatigable, working around the clock to help me meet publisher's deadlines. With unfailing good spirits she managed successive crises and kept my office under control.

Without my agent, Raphael Sagalyn, there might not have been a book. He urged me to move my work on *Getting Past No* from the back burner to the front, provided valuable feedback, and put me together with Bantam.

Bantam's fine team improved the book considerably. It has been a privilege to work with Genevieve Young, the superlative editor who took the time to coach and coax me through endless drafts. Danelle McCafferty, my line editor, applied her skillful pencil to the finished manuscript and cheered me along through the last stretch. Betsy Cenedella provided meticulous copy editing.

Let me end with a personal note. Shortly before I began writing this book, I had the great fortune to meet Elizabeth Sherwood. Little did I realize that she came from a family of determined and devoted editors. Dorothy, Richard, and Benjamin Sherwood marked up each successive draft with skill and savvy. Elizabeth read the book aloud with me from start to finish, making it leaner and more lucid. My greatest debt is to her: Her love and support got me past *Getting Past No.*

WILLIAM L. URY
January 1991
Santa Fe, New Mexico

PART I

Getting Ready

Overview

BREAKING THROUGH BARRIERS TO COOPERATION

Diplomacy is the art of letting someone else have your way.

—*Daniele Vare, Italian diplomat*

We all negotiate every day. Much of our time is spent trying to reach agreement with others. We may try to negotiate in a cooperative spirit but frequently we find ourselves frustrated. *We* want to get to yes, but often the answer we get back is NO.

Think of a typical day: Over breakfast you may get into an argument with your spouse about buying a new car. You think it's time, but your spouse says, "Don't be ridiculous! You know we can't afford it right now." You arrive at work for a morning meeting with your boss. You present a carefully prepared proposal for a new project, but your boss interrupts you after a minute and says: "We already tried that and it didn't work. Next item."

During your lunch hour you try to return a defective

toaster-oven, but the salesperson refuses to refund your money because you don't have the sales slip: "It's store policy."

In the afternoon you bring an already-agreed-upon contract to a client for his signature. You have trumpeted the deal to your associates and made the necessary arrangements with manufacturing. But your client tells you: "I'm sorry. My boss refuses to okay the purchase unless you give us a fifteen percent discount."

In the evening you need to return some phone calls, but the line is tied up by your thirteen-year-old. Exasperated, you say, "Get off the phone." The teenager shouts down the hall, "Why don't you get me my own phone line? All my friends have them!"

Each of us faces tough negotiations with an irritable spouse, a domineering boss, a rigid salesperson, a tricky customer, or an impossible teenager. Under stress, even nice, reasonable people can turn into angry, intractable opponents. Negotiations can bog down or break down, consuming our time, keeping us awake at night, and giving us ulcers.

Broadly defined, negotiation is the process of back-and-forth communication aimed at reaching agreement with others when some of your interests are shared and some are opposed. Negotiation is not limited to the activity of formally sitting across a table discussing a contentious issue; it is the informal activity you engage in whenever you try to get something you want from another person.

Think for a moment about how you make important decisions in your life—the decisions that have the greatest impact on your performance at work and your satisfaction at home. How many of those decisions can you make unilaterally and how many do you have to reach with others—through negotiation? Most people I ask this question answer: "I have to negotiate almost all of them." Negotiation is the pre-eminent form of decision-making in personal and professional life.

It is also increasingly the most important means of making decisions in the public arena. Even if we aren't personally sitting at the table, our lives are affected by the outcome of negotiations. When talks between the school board and teachers' union break down and the teachers go on strike, our children end up staying home from school. When negotiations between our business and a potential purchaser fall through and the business goes bankrupt, we may lose our jobs. When discussions between our government and its adversaries come to naught, the result may be war. In sum, negotiations shape our lives.

Joint Problem-Solving

We may all be negotiators, yet many of us don't like to negotiate. We see negotiation as stressful confrontation. We see ourselves faced with an unpleasant choice. If we are "soft" in order to preserve the relationship, we end up giving up our position. If we are "hard" in order to win our position, we strain the relationship or perhaps lose it altogether.

There is an alternative: joint problem-solving. It is neither exclusively soft nor hard, but a combination of each. It is *soft on the people, hard on the problem.* Instead of attacking each other, you jointly attack the problem. Instead of glowering across the table, you sit next to each other facing your common problem. In short, you turn face-to-face confrontation into side-by-side problem-solving. This is the kind of negotiation Roger Fisher and I described more than a decade ago in our book *Getting to Yes*.

Joint problem-solving revolves around *interests* instead of positions. You begin by identifying each side's interests—the concerns, needs, fears, and desires that underlie and motivate your opposing positions. You then explore different options for meeting those interests. Your goal is to reach a mutually satisfactory agreement in an efficient and amicable fashion.

If you are looking for a promotion and raise, for example, and your boss says there's no money in the budget, the negotiation doesn't stop there. It becomes an exercise in joint problem-solving. Your boss inquires about your interests, which may be to pay your children's tuition and to grow in your job. You brainstorm together about how to satisfy these interests while staying within the budget. You may end up agreeing on a new set of responsibilities, a tuition loan from the company, and the promise of a raise next year to pay back the loan. Your basic interests are satisfied; so are your employer's.

Joint problem-solving can generate better results for both sides. It saves time and energy by cutting out the posturing. And it usually leads to better working relationships and to mutual benefit in the future.

Five Barriers to Cooperation

Skeptics are quick to point out that all this is easy to say, but hard to do. The principles of joint problem-solving, they say, are like marriage vows of mutual support and

The Goal: JOINT PROBLEM-SOLVING	BARRIERS TO COOPERATION	Strategy: BREAKTHROUGH NEGOTIATION
• People Sitting Side by Side	• Your Reaction • Their Emotion	• Go to the Balcony • Step to Their Side
• Facing the Problem	• Their Position	• Reframe
• Reaching a Mutually Satisfactory Agreement	• Their Dissatisfaction • Their Power	• Build Them a Golden Bridge • Use Power to Educate

fidelity: They no doubt produce more satisfying relationships, but they are hard to apply in the real world of stresses and strains, temptations and tempests.

At the start, you may try to get your opponent to tackle the problem jointly, but instead you may find yourselves in a face-to-face confrontation. It is all too easy to get drawn into a ferocious emotional battle, to fall back into the familiar routine of adopting rigid positions, or to let the other side take advantage of you.

There are real-world barriers that get in the way of cooperation. The five most common ones are:

Your reaction. The first barrier lies within you. Human beings are reaction machines. When you're under stress, or when you encounter a NO, or feel you are being attacked, you naturally feel like striking back. Usually this just perpetuates the action-reaction cycle that leaves both sides losers. Or, alternatively, you may react by impulsively giving in just to end the negotiation and preserve the relationship. You lose and, having demonstrated your weakness, you expose yourself to exploitation by others. The problem you thus face in negotiation is not only the other side's difficult behavior but your own reaction, which can easily perpetuate that behavior.

Their emotion. The next barrier is the other side's negative emotions. Behind their attacks may lie anger and hostility. Behind their rigid positions may lie fear and distrust. Convinced they are right and you are wrong, they may refuse to listen. Seeing the world as eat-or-be-eaten, they may feel justified in using nasty tactics.

Their position. In joint problem-solving, you face the problem and attack it together. The barrier in the way is the other side's positional behavior: their habit of digging into a position and trying to get you to give in. Often they know no other way to negotiate. They are merely using the conventional negotiating tactics they first learned in the sandbox. In their eyes, the only alternative is for *them* to give in—and they certainly don't want to do that.

Their dissatisfaction. Your goal may be to reach a mutually satisfactory agreement, but you may find the other side not at all interested in such an outcome. They may not see *how* it will benefit them. Even if you can satisfy their interests, they may fear losing face if they have to back down. And if it is *your* idea, they may reject it for that reason alone.

Their power. Finally, if the other side sees the negotiation as a win-lose proposition, they will be determined to beat you. They may be guided by the precept "What's mine is mine. What's yours is negotiable." If they can get what they want by power plays, why should they cooperate with you?

Getting past no requires breaking through each of these five barriers to cooperation: your reaction, their emotion, their position, their dissatisfaction, and their power. It is easy to believe that stonewalling, attacks, and tricks are just part of the other side's basic nature, and that there is little you can do to change such difficult behavior. But you *can* affect this behavior if you can deal successfully with its underlying motivations.

The Breakthrough Strategy

This book lays out a five-step strategy for breaking through each of these five barriers—the strategy of *breakthrough negotiation*.

An analogy from sailing will help explain this strategy.

In sailing, you rarely if ever get to your destination by heading straight for it. In between you and your goal are strong winds and tides, reefs and shoals, not to speak of storms and squalls. To get where you want to go, you need to tack—to zigzag your way toward your destination.

The same is true in the world of negotiation. Your desired destination is a mutually satisfactory agreement. The direct route—focusing first on interests and then developing options that satisfy those interests—seems straightforward and easy. But in the real world of strong reactions and emotions, rigid positions, powerful dissatisfactions and aggressions, you often cannot get to a mutually satisfactory agreement by the direct route. Instead, you need to navigate past no by tacking—taking an indirect route.

The essence of the breakthrough strategy is *indirect action*. It requires you to do the opposite of what you naturally feel like doing in difficult situations. When the other side stonewalls or attacks, you may feel like responding in kind. Confronted with hostility, you may argue. Confronted with unreasonable positions, you may reject. Confronted with intransigence, you may push. Confronted with aggression, you may escalate. But this just leaves you frustrated, playing the other side's game by *their* rules.

Your single greatest opportunity as a negotiator is to *change the game*. Instead of playing their way, let them have *your* way—the way of joint problem-solving. The great home-run hitter Sadahara Oh, the Japanese equivalent of Babe Ruth, once explained his batting secret. Oh said that he looked on the opposing pitcher as his *partner*, who with every pitch was serving up an *opportunity* for him to hit a home run. Breakthrough negotiators do the same: They treat their opponents as negotiating partners who are presenting an opportunity to reach a mutually satisfactory agreement.

As in the Japanese martial arts of judo, jujitsu, and aikido, you need to avoid pitting your strength directly against your opponent's. Since efforts to break down the other side's resistance usually only increase it, you try to go around their resistance. That is the way to break through.

Breakthrough negotiation is the opposite of imposing your position on the other side. Rather than pounding in a new idea from the outside, you encourage them to reach for it from within. Rather than telling them what to do, you let them figure it out. Rather than pressuring them to change their mind, you create an environment in which they can learn. Only *they* can break through their own resistance; *your* job is to *help* them.

Their resistance to joint problem-solving stems from the five barriers described above. Your job as a breakthrough negotiator is to clear away the barriers that lie between their NO and the YES of a mutually satisfactory agreement. For each of the five barriers, there is a corresponding step in the strategy:

Step One. Since the first barrier is your natural reaction, the first step involves suspending that reaction. To engage in joint problem-solving, you need to regain your mental balance and stay focused on achieving what you want. A useful image for getting perspective on the situation is to imagine yourself standing on a balcony looking down on your negotiation. The first step in the breakthrough strategy is to *Go to the Balcony*.

Step Two. The next barrier for you to overcome is the other side's negative emotions—their defensiveness, fear, suspicion, and hostility. It is all too easy to get drawn into an argument, but you need to resist this temptation. Just as you've regained your mental balance, you need to help the other side regain *theirs*. To create the right climate for joint problem-solving, you need to defuse their negative emotions. To do this, you need to do the opposite of what they expect. They expect you to behave like an adversary. Instead, you should take their side by listening to them, acknowledging their points and their feelings, agreeing with them, and showing them respect. If you want to sit side by side facing the problem, you will need to *Step to Their Side*.

Step Three. Now you want to tackle the problem together. This is hard to do, however, when the other side digs into their position and tries to get you to give in. It's natural to feel like rejecting their position, but this will only lead them to dig in further. So do the opposite. Accept whatever they say and reframe it as an attempt to deal with the problem. For example, take their position and probe behind it: "Tell me more. Help me understand *why* you want that." Act as if they were your partners genuinely interested in solving the problem. The third step in the breakthrough strategy is to *Reframe*.

Step Four. While you may now have engaged the other side in joint problem-solving, you may still be far from reaching a mutually satisfactory agreement. The other side may be dissatisfied, unconvinced of the benefits of agreement. You may feel like pushing them, but this will only make them more resistant. So do the opposite. In the words of the Chinese sage, "build a golden bridge" from their position to a mutually satisfactory solution. You need to bridge the gap between their interests and yours. You need to help them save face and make the outcome look like a victory for them. The fourth step is to *Build Them a Golden Bridge*.

Step Five. Despite your best efforts, the other side may still refuse to cooperate, believing they can beat you at the power game. You may be tempted at this point to escalate. Threats and coercion often backfire, however, and lead to costly and futile battles. The alternative is to use power not to escalate, but to educate. Enhance your negotiating power and use it to bring them back to the table. Show them that they cannot win by themselves but only together with you. The fifth step is to *Use Power to Educate*.

The sequence of the steps is important. You cannot defuse the other side's negative emotions unless you have controlled your own. It is hard to build them a golden bridge unless you have changed the game to joint problem-solving. This does not mean that once you have taken one step, you have completed it. On the contrary, you need to keep going to the balcony throughout the negotiation. As the other side's anger and frustration resurface, you need to keep stepping to their side. The process is like a symphony in which the different instruments join in sequentially and then play their parts throughout.

Breakthrough negotiation can be used with anyone— an irascible boss, a temperamental teenager, a hostile co-worker, or an impossible customer. It can be used by diplomats trying to stave off a war, lawyers trying to avoid a costly court battle, or spouses trying to keep a marriage together.

Because every person and every situation is different, you will need to marry the five breakthrough principles with your own knowledge of the particulars in order to create a strategy that works for you. There is no magic recipe that will guarantee your success in every negotiation. But with patience, persistence, *and* the breakthrough strategy, you can maximize your chances of getting what you want in even the most difficult negotiations.

The chapters that follow explain the five breakthrough steps and present specific techniques for carrying them out, illustrating their application with concrete examples. First, however, you will find a prologue about the key to effective negotiation: preparation.

Prologue

PREPARE, PREPARE, PREPARE

I once asked Lord Caradon, a British diplomat, what was the most valuable lesson he had learned during his long and distinguished service in government. "The most valuable lesson," he replied, "I learned at the very start of my career when I was posted to the Middle East as an assistant to a local administrator. My superior would visit a different village each day dealing with disputes and other pressing matters. Once he arrived, pandemonium broke out as people besieged him with requests and offered him coffee. It wouldn't cease until he left at sunset. He might easily have forgotten his objectives but for one simple habit.

"Just before he entered the village in the morning, he would pull the jeep off to the side of the road and ask, 'What is it that we want to leave this village tonight having achieved?' He and I would answer the question, then we would go into the village. When we left that evening, he would again pull the jeep off the road and ask, 'Now, did we get it? Did we achieve what we set out to do?'"

That simple habit of mind was the most valuable lesson Caradon had ever learned. Before every meeting, prepare. After every meeting, assess your progress, adapt your strategy, and prepare again. The secret of effective negotiation is that simple: prepare, prepare, prepare.

Most negotiations are won or lost even before the talking begins, depending on the quality of the preparation. People who think they can "wing it" without preparing often find themselves sadly mistaken. Even if they reach agreement, they may miss opportunities for joint gain they might well have come across in preparing. There is no substitute for effective preparation. The more difficult the negotiation, the more intensive your preparation needs to be.

When it comes to preparation, many people throw up their hands and say, "But I can't afford the *time* to prepare." Preparation time tends to be the last thing on the "to do" list. There always seems to be an urgent phone call to return, an important meeting to attend, or a household crisis to manage.

The truth is that you can't afford *not* to prepare. Take the time even if it means taking time out of the actual negotiation itself. Negotiations would be a lot more effective if people spent more of their limited time preparing and less in actual meetings.

It is true that most of us operate under fairly severe time constraints. The preparation guidelines outlined below take that into account. They can be accomplished in as little as fifteen minutes.* If you want a rule of thumb, think about preparing a minute for every minute of interaction with the other side.

How should you prepare? When you're embarking on

---

*For a quick preparation, a one-page preparation worksheet is provided for you on p. 173 at the end of the book.

a negotiation, just as on a voyage, the first thing you need is a good map.

Mapping Out the Way to Agreement

There are five important points along the way to a mutually satisfactory agreement: *interests, options* for satisfying those interests, *standards* for resolving differences fairly, *alternatives* to negotiation, and *proposals* for agreement.

1. Interests

Negotiation typically begins when one side's position comes into conflict with the other side's. In conventional bargaining, your position may be all you need to know in advance. But joint problem-solving revolves around the interests that lie behind each side's positions. The distinction is critical: Your position is the concrete things you say you want—the dollars and cents, the terms and conditions. Your interests are the intangible motivations that lead you to take that position—your needs, desires, concerns, fears, and aspirations. In order to end up with an agreement that satisfies both sides, you need to begin by figuring out each side's interests.

Figure out your interests. Unless you know where you want to go, you're unlikely to get there. In a negotiation with a difficult client who insists on sticking to the original fee for your services despite the unforeseen additional work required, your position may be, "I want a thirty percent increase in fees to reflect the additional work." Your interests in wanting the fee increase may be to preserve your profit margin while keeping the client happy. You uncover your interests by asking the simple question *Why?* "Why do I want that? What problem am I trying to solve?"

It's important to rank your interests so that you don't make the all-too-common mistake of trading off an important interest for a less important one. If the relationship with the client promises to be a very profitable one, you may want to make that the number-one priority. Your interest in realizing a profit on the immediate project may be the second interest, and the third may be avoiding setting a precedent of doing extra work without compensation.

Figure out their interests. Negotiation is a two-way street. You usually can't satisfy *your* interests unless you also satisfy the other side's. It is therefore just as important to understand their interests as your own. Your difficult client may be concerned about sticking within an established budget and looking good to their boss.

I remember my uncle Mel once coming to visit me at my Harvard Law School office when he returned to campus for his twenty-fifth alumni reunion. At one point he took me aside and said: "You know, Bill, it has taken me twenty-five years to unlearn what I learned at Harvard Law School. Because what I learned at Harvard Law School is that all that counts in life are the *facts*—who's right and who's wrong. It's taken me twenty-five years to learn that just as important as the facts, if not more important, are people's *perceptions* of those facts. Unless you understand their perspective, you're never going to be effective at making deals or settling disputes."

The single most important skill in negotiation is the ability to put yourself in the other side's shoes. If you are trying to change their thinking, you need to begin by understanding what their thinking is.

How can you learn about the other side's interests? Try the simple exercise of imagining from *their* point of view what they seem to care most about. Then ask yourself: Do they often behave in a difficult fashion or is this just a temporary aberration? What has been happening in their personal or professional lives that may be coloring their attitude toward you? Do they have a reputation for honesty and fair dealing? If you have time, you might talk to people who know them—their friends and peers, their customers and employees. The more you can find out about the other side, the better your chances of influencing them successfully.

2. Options

The purpose of identifying each side's interests is to see if you can devise creative options to satisfy them. An option is a possible agreement or part of an agreement. Inventing options for mutual gain is a negotiator's single greatest opportunity. Effective negotiators do not just divvy up a fixed pie. They first explore how to expand the pie.

While it may not be possible to obtain your position, it is often possible to satisfy your interests. You may not succeed in obtaining the thirty percent fee increase, but you may invent an option that allows you to realize a profit on the project while keeping your client satisfied. Could you transfer some of the additional work required to your client's staff? Could you stretch out the project into the next fiscal year so the additional fees come out of next year's budget? Could you take a cut in compensation this year for a specific commitment to significant future work? Could you show your client that this additional work will result in substantial savings, part of which could be used to pay for the additional work?

A common mistake in negotiation is to dwell on a single solution, your original position. By opening yourself up to consideration of a multitude of options, you may generate new possibilities, one of which might meet your interests while also satisfying the other side's.

The biggest obstacle in the way of generating creative options is a little voice in the back of our heads that is always saying, "That won't work!" Criticism and evaluation, while important functions, interfere with your imagination. It is better to separate the two functions. Invent first, evaluate later. Suspend judgment for a few minutes and try to come up with as many ideas as possible. Include ideas that at first seem like wild ideas, remembering that many of the best ideas in the world started out as wild ideas everyone disparaged. After brainstorming a multitude of options, you can review them and evaluate how well they satisfy your interests—and the other side's too.

3. Standards

Once you have expanded the pie, you need to think about how to divide it up. How will you jointly select an option with the other side when your interests are opposed? Your client wants to pay less for your work; you would like them to pay more. How do you resolve the issue?

Perhaps the most common method is to use a contest of wills. Each side insists on its position, trying to get the other to give in. The problem is that nobody likes to give in. A contest of wills thus quickly becomes a conflict of egos. The person who eventually gives in remembers it and tries to even the score the next time—*if* there is a next time.

Successful negotiators head off a contest of wills by turning the selection process into a joint search for a fair and mutually satisfactory solution. They rely heavily on fair standards independent of either side's will. An independent standard is a measuring stick that allows you to decide what is a fair solution. Common standards are market value, equal treatment, the law, or simply the way the issue has been resolved before.

The great virtue of standards is that, instead of one side giving in to the other on a particular point, both can defer to what seems fair. It is easier for your client to accept a standard like market rate than it is to pay a certain fee just because *you* say that's what you charge.

So think in advance about what standards you could appeal to in your negotiation. Do your homework on market rates, scientific criteria, costs, technical measures, and precedents. Come armed to persuade.

4. Alternatives

All too often people go into a negotiation looking for agreement and examine their alternatives only if things go badly. This is a classic mistake. Knowing what your alternatives are can determine your success in satisfying your interests.

The purpose of negotiation is *not* always to reach agreement. For agreement is only a means to an end, and that end is to satisfy your interests. The purpose of negotiation is to explore whether you can satisfy your interests better through an agreement than you could by pursuing your Best Alternative to a Negotiated Agreement (BATNA).

Your BATNA is your walkaway alternative. It's your

best course of action for satisfying your interests *without* the other's agreement. If you're negotiating with your boss over a raise, your BATNA might be to find a job with another firm. If you're negotiating with a salesperson, your BATNA might be to talk to the store manager or, if that fails, you might go to another store. If one nation is negotiating with another over unfair trade practices, its BATNA may be to appeal to the appropriate international tribunal. Usually resorting to your alternative entails costs to you and to the relationship, which is why you are negotiating to develop a better solution.

BATNA is the key to negotiating power. Your power depends less on whether you are bigger, stronger, more senior, or richer than the other person than on how good your BATNA is. If you have a viable alternative, then you have leverage in the negotiation. The better your BATNA, the more power you have.

Identify your BATNA. Your BATNA should be your measuring stick for evaluating any potential agreement. To identify your BATNA, you should consider three kinds of alternatives. First, what can you do all by yourself to pursue your interests? Your "walkaway" alternative may be to find another supplier if you're a buyer or another customer if you're a seller.

Second, what can you do directly to the other side to make them respect your interests? Your "interactive" alternative may be to go on strike or to go to war. Third, how can you bring a third party into the situation to further your interests? Your "third-party" alternative may be to resort to mediation, arbitration, or court. After generating a set of possible alternatives, select the one that is most likely to satisfy your interests.

Keep your BATNA in your pocket. When you're under

heavy attack and feel panicky, you can pat your pocket and say to yourself, "I'm okay if it doesn't go okay."

Boost your BATNA. A good BATNA usually does not already exist; it needs to be developed. If your BATNA is not very strong, you should take steps to improve it. For instance, don't just identify your BATNA as seeking another job in the same industry. Go to the trouble of getting an actual job offer. If you are selling your house, don't stop showing it just because one person has indicated serious interest; keep looking for another potential buyer. Or, if your company is at risk of being taken over by a corporate raider, look for friendly buyers or consider borrowing money to take your company private.

Decide if you should negotiate. Once you've formulated your BATNA, you should ask yourself, "Should I negotiate at all?" Have you ever wondered why some people keep trying to negotiate with an abusive boss long after they should have left the job? Or why frustrated parents will continue to make deals with their rebellious teenagers, each pact broken as quickly as the last? Habit, guilt, self-blame, and fear may all play a role, but often the central reason is that the employee or parents have lost sight of their best alternative. If they thought about it, they might well discover that there was a better way to satisfy their interests that didn't depend on having to negotiate with their nemesis.

Perhaps your BATNA *is* better than any agreement you could reach with the other person. Remember, too, that the negotiation process itself is not free of costs. It can take a lot of time and effort, in the course of which your other alternatives may vanish. Your decision to negotiate should therefore be a carefully considered one.

Keep in mind that it is easy to overestimate how good

your BATNA is. Many business executives, listening to the advice of overconfident lawyers, have eschewed negotiations and taken a dispute to court, only to find themselves on the path to financial ruin. In any lawsuit, strike, or war, one contender—and often two—discover that their BATNA wasn't as good as they imagined. Knowing in advance that your alternative is unattractive ought to make you work hard to reach an agreement.

Identify **their** *BATNA.* Knowing the other side's BATNA can be just as important as knowing your own. It gives you an idea of the challenge you face: developing an agreement that is superior to their best alternative. It helps you avoid the dual mistakes of underestimating how good it is and overestimating how good it is. Your BATNA may be weak, but the other side's BATNA may be weak too. Many salespeople and consultants are convinced their clients can just switch to the competition in a flash. They often fail to appreciate the true costs of changing vendors. An objective look at their clients' BATNA can give them more confidence in a difficult negotiation.

If the other side's BATNA is to use coercion, you can prepare in advance to counter it. If your company is in danger from a corporate raider, for example, you can pass corporate bylaws that would render a hostile takeover more difficult. Think about how to neutralize the effect on you of the other side's coercive actions.

5. Proposals

Your work on interests and options opens up the problem for a creative solution. Your work on fair standards and alternatives helps you select an appropriate option to shape into a proposal for possible agreement.

To formulate a solid proposal, you want to select an option that satisfies your interests well, certainly better than your BATNA could. The option should also meet the other side's interests better than you think their BATNA could, and should be based, if possible, on fair standards. What distinguishes a proposal from a simple option is commitment: A proposal is a possible agreement to which you are ready to say yes.

Of course, there may be more than one possible agreement that meets all these criteria. Indeed, it is useful to have three proposals in mind:

What do you aspire to? Many of us tend to adopt rather modest goals, wishing to avoid "failing." Unfortunately, low aspirations tend to be self-fulfilling. What you don't ask for, the other side is unlikely to give you. Not surprisingly, those who begin with realistically high aspirations often end up with better agreements. How high is realistic? "Realistic" means within the bounds set by fairness and by the other side's best alternative. Aim high.

So begin by asking yourself: "What agreement do I aspire to? What would genuinely satisfy my interests and at the same time meet enough of the other side's basic concerns that there is at least a chance that they would agree?"

What would you be content with? Often you may not get everything you would like. It is therefore useful to ask yourself a second question: "What agreement, perhaps far from perfect, would still satisfy my basic interests sufficiently that I would be reasonably content?"

What could you live with? The third proposal should be based directly on your assessment of your BATNA: "What

agreement would satisfy my interests only marginally better than my BATNA could? What agreement could I live
with, but just barely?" If you can't in the end obtain an
agreement at least as good as that, you should consider
walking away from the table and resorting to your alternative. This proposal will function like a trip wire, re-
minding you that you are in danger of accepting an
agreement worse for you than your BATNA.

Think of these three proposals not as rigid positions
but as concrete illustrations of the kinds of outcomes that
would satisfy your interests. You cannot know for certain
that the other side will agree to your proposals. And you
may learn something in the course of the negotiation that
will enable you to come up with a solution that meets
your interests—and theirs—even better.

Rehearse

Preparation is easier to do when you're talking it over with
someone else. Others bring new perspectives, compel you
to address points of difficulty that you might otherwise
avoid, and offer you moral encouragement. So think about
scheduling a preparation session with a colleague or friend.
It has the added advantage of ensuring that you do prepare.

In your session, consider rehearsing what you will say
to the other side and how you will respond to what they
say. After all, lawyers rehearse tough cases, politicians rehearse tough media interviews, executives rehearse tough
presentations to stockholders—why shouldn't you rehearse a tough negotiation? The best place to make mistakes is in rehearsing with a friend or colleague, not in
negotiating for real.

So ask your colleague to play the role of the other side for a few minutes and try out your powers of persuasion, focusing on interests, options, and standards. After you have finished, ask your colleague to tell you what worked and what didn't. What did it feel like to be on the receiving end of your words? What should you do differently? And then try it out again until you get it right. If you don't have a colleague or friend to rehearse with, try writing out what you plan to say and rehearse by yourself.

Anticipate what tactics the other side may try and think in advance of how best to respond. Having prepared in advance, you are less likely to be caught by surprise. Instead you can say to yourself, "Ah! I knew that was coming" and deliver your prepared response. That is the value of preparation.

Preparing to Navigate

Ideally you would now conduct a negotiation in the same way that you have prepared. You would begin by exploring interests, trying to understand what each side is genuinely concerned about. Then you would discuss various options without commitment, seeing if you could genuinely satisfy both sides' interests. You would consider different standards of fairness for reconciling your differences. Finally you would exchange proposals back and forth in an effort to reach a mutually satisfactory agreement that in any case is better for each side than resorting to your respective BATNAs.

In the real world, however, your efforts to engage in

joint problem-solving run up against powerful reactions, hostile emotions, rigid positions, strong dissatisfactions, and aggressive power plays. Your challenge is to change the game from face-to-face confrontation into side-by-side problem-solving, turning your opponent into a negotiating partner. Now that you have a good map of where you want to go, you need to use the breakthrough strategy to navigate past the obstacles that stand in your way. The next five chapters are intended to prepare you to navigate.

PART II

Using the Breakthrough Strategy

1

Don't React:

GO TO THE BALCONY

Speak when you are angry and you will make the best speech you will ever regret.

—*Ambrose Bierce*

If you watch the negotiations going on around you, you will see countless instances in which people react to each other without thinking. Too many negotiations proceed like this:

HUSBAND (*thinking he is focused on the problem*): Honey, we've got to do something about the house. It's a mess.
WIFE (*perceiving this as a personal attack*): You don't lift a finger! You don't even do the things you promise. Last night—
HUSBAND (*interrupting*): I know. I know. It's just that—
WIFE (*not listening*):—you said you'd take out the garbage. I had to do it this morning.

HUSBAND *(trying to return to the problem)*: Don't get defensive. I was just trying to point out that we're both—

WIFE *(not listening)*: And it was your turn to take the kids to school.

HUSBAND *(reacting)*: Come on! I told you I had a breakfast meeting this morning.

WIFE *(beginning to shout)*: Oh, so your time is more important than mine, is it? I have a job too! I'm sick and tired of playing second fiddle in this band.

HUSBAND *(beginning to shout)*: Give me a break! Who's paying most of the bills around here?

Neither the husband's interest in a clean house nor the wife's interest in more help is advanced by this exchange. But that doesn't stop either spouse from going at the other. Action provokes reaction, reaction provokes counterreaction, and on it goes in an endless argument. The same pattern repeats itself when business partners quarrel about who gets the corner office, when union and management officials wrestle over work rules, or when ethnic groups battle over territory.

Three Natural Reactions

Human beings are reaction machines. The most natural thing to do when confronted with a difficult situation is to react—to act without thinking. There are three common reactions:

Striking Back

When the other side attacks you, your instinctive reaction is to attack right back, to "fight fire with fire" and "give them a taste of their own medicine." If they take a rigid and extreme position, you do the same.

Occasionally, this shows them that two can play the same game and makes them stop. More often, however, this strategy lands you in a futile and costly confrontation. You provide them with a justification for their unreasonable behavior. They think: "Ah, I knew that you were out to get me. This proves it." Escalation often follows in the form of a shouting match, a corporate showdown, a lawsuit, or a war.

Take the example of the senior manager who had developed a new information system for his company's manufacturing process. To implement it he needed the agreement of all the plant managers across the country. Everyone agreed except for the manager of the largest plant in Dallas, who told him: "I don't want your people fooling around in my business. The only way things get done around here is if I'm in control. I can do the job better on my own." Frustrated, the systems manager reacted by threatening to take the matter to the company president, but that only enraged the plant manager. The end result: The systems manager's appeal to the company president backfired, since it implied the manager couldn't work smoothly with peers. What's more, the president refused to intervene, and the new information system languished on the drawing table.

Striking back rarely advances your immediate interests and usually damages your long-term relationships. Even if you do win the battle, you may lose the war.

The other problem with striking back is that people who play hardball are usually very good at it. They may actually be hoping that you are going to attack them. If you do, you put yourself on their home turf, playing the game the way they like to play it.

Giving In

The opposite of striking back is giving in. The other side may succeed in making you feel so uncomfortable with the negotiation that you give in just to be done with it. They pressure you, implying that you are the one who is blocking agreement. Do you really want to be the one responsible for dragging out the negotiations, disrupting the relationship, missing the opportunity of a lifetime? Wouldn't it just be better to say yes?

Many of us make agreements only to wake up the next morning slapping our foreheads and exclaiming, "How could I have been so stupid! What did I agree to?" Many of us sign contracts—for example, when buying a car—without reading all the fine print. Why? Because the salesperson is leaning over us, the kids are eagerly waiting to drive home in the new car, and we're afraid of looking stupid if we ask questions about the contract, which is totally incomprehensible anyway.

Giving in usually results in an unsatisfactory outcome. You feel "had." Moreover, it rewards the other side for bad behavior and gives you a reputation for weakness that they—and others—may try to exploit in the future. Just as giving in to a child's temper tantrum only reinforces this behavior pattern, so, too, giving in to an angry person only encourages angry outbursts in the future. Our boss's and client's terrible tempers may appear to be uncontrollable—but a temper *can* be controlled. They probably don't throw tantrums in front of *their* bosses.

Sometimes we are intimidated and appease unreasonable people under the illusion that if we give in just this one last time, we will get them off our back and will never have to deal with them again. All too often, however, such people come back for further concessions. There is a saying that an appeaser is someone who believes that if you keep on throwing steaks to a tiger, the tiger will eventually become a vegetarian.

Breaking Off

A third common reaction is to break off relations with the difficult person or organization. If it's a marriage, we get a divorce. If it's a job, we resign. If we are involved in a joint venture, we dissolve it.

At times, avoidance is a perfectly appropriate strategy. Sometimes it is better to end a personal or business relationship if continuing means being taken advantage of or getting into fights again and again. Sometimes, too, breaking off reminds the other side of their stake in the relationship and leads them to act more reasonably.

But the costs—both financial and emotional—of breaking off the relationship are often high: a lost client, a career setback, a shattered family. Breaking off is frequently a hasty reaction that we come to regret later. We all know people who take a job or enter a personal relationship, become frustrated with their boss or partner, and then leave without giving it a chance. Often they misinterpret the other person's behavior and do not try to work it out. A pattern of breaking off relationships means you never get anywhere because you are always starting over.

The Dangers of Reacting

In reacting, we lose sight of our interests. Consider the Pentagon's reaction to the Iranian hostage crisis of 1979–81. Shortly after the crisis began, a news reporter asked a Pentagon spokesperson what the armed forces were doing to help. The spokesperson answered that there was not much they could do without jeopardizing the lives of the American hostages. The Pentagon, he continued, was working on tough measures to be carried out *after* the hostages were released. But he wasn't thinking clearly: Why would the Iranian students release the hostages if they believed that the United States would retaliate soon afterward? The Pentagon made the all-too-common mistake of confusing getting even with getting what you want.

Often the other side is actually trying to make you react. The first casualty of an attack is your objectivity—the faculty you need most to negotiate effectively. They are trying to throw you off balance and prevent you from thinking straight. They are trying to bait you like a fish so that they can control you. When you react, you are hooked.

Much of your opponent's power derives from the ability to make you react. Have you ever wondered how a small terrorist group in the Middle East can command worldwide attention and create sleepless nights for the leader of the most powerful nation on earth—simply by nabbing a passing American on the street? The hostage-takers have hardly any power in and of themselves—their power comes from the reaction of the American public.

Even if reacting doesn't lead to a gross error on your part, it feeds the unproductive cycle of action and reaction. Ask the wife why she shouts at her husband and she may answer, "Because *he* shouts at me." Ask the husband and he will give the same answer: "Because *she* shouts at me." By reacting, you become part of the problem. Just as it takes two to tango, it takes two to tangle.

Go to the Balcony

If the bad news is that you contribute to the vicious cycle of action and reaction, the good news is that you have the power to break the cycle at any time—*unilaterally*. How? By *not* reacting. In physics class we learn that "for every action, there is an equal and opposite reaction." Newton's law, however, applies to objects, not minds. *Objects react. Minds can choose not to.*

O. Henry's story "The Ransom of Red Chief" offers a fictional example of the power of not reacting. When their son was kidnapped, the parents chose not to respond to the kidnappers' demands. As time passed, the boy became such a burden to the kidnappers that they offered to pay the parents to take him back. The story illustrates the psychological game that depends on your reacting. By refusing to react, the parents thwarted the kidnappers' plans.

When you find yourself facing a difficult negotiation, you need to step back, collect your wits, and see the situation objectively. Imagine you are negotiating on a stage

and then imagine yourself climbing onto a balcony overlooking the stage. The "balcony" is a metaphor for a mental
attitude of detachment. From the balcony you can calmly
evaluate the conflict almost as if you were a third party.
You can think constructively for both sides and look for a
mutually satisfactory way to resolve the problem.

In the ancient Japanese art of swordsmanship, students
were instructed to look at an opponent as if he were a far-
off mountain. Musashi, the greatest samurai of all, called
this a "distanced view of close things." Such is the view
from the balcony.

Going to the balcony means distancing yourself from
your natural impulses and emotions. Consider the case of
a film executive named Janet Jenkins, who was winding
up a multimillion-dollar sale of programming to a cable
TV network. An hour into her final meeting with the network negotiator, the head of the network stormed in. He
attacked Janet's product and her personal integrity and
demanded radical changes in the deal. Instead of reacting,
however, Janet controlled her emotions and went to her
mental balcony. She realized that defending herself or
counterattacking would only add fuel to the fire and would
not bring her any closer to clinching the deal. So she simply
heard the network chairman out. After he finished and
left the room, Janet excused herself for a minute, osten-
sibly to make a phone call but actually to recover her mental
balance.

When she returned, the network negotiator looked up
and asked, "Now, shall we pick up our conversation where
we left off?" He was saying, in other words, "Discount what
the chairman said. He was just blowing off steam. Let's get
back to business." If Janet had reacted, the negotiation
would have gone way off course. Because she had gone to
the balcony instead, she was able to proceed smoothly to
conclude the deal.

You ought to go to the balcony before the negotiation even begins—in order to prepare. And you should go to the balcony at every possible opportunity throughout the negotiation. At all times, you will be tempted to react impulsively to your opponent's difficult behavior. But at all times, you need to keep your eyes on the prize.

The prize is an agreement that satisfies your interests, certainly better than your BATNA could. It must also meet the other person's interests acceptably. Once you have an idea of what the prize looks like, your challenge is to stay focused on obtaining it. This is not easy. When you feel angry and defensive, you feel like striking out. When you're frustrated and fearful, you feel like walking away. How can you suspend your natural reactions?

Name the Game

Often you don't even realize you are reacting, because you are too enmeshed in the situation. The first task, therefore, is to recognize the tactic. In ancient mythology, calling an evil spirit by its name enabled you to ward it off. So, too, with unfair tactics—identify them and you break the spell they cast.

Three Kinds of Tactics

There are dozens of tactics, but they can be grouped into three general categories, depending on whether they are obstructive, offensive, or deceptive:

Stone walls. A stone-wall tactic is a refusal to budge. The other side may try to convince you that they have no flexibility and that there is no choice other than their position. Stone walls can take the form of a *fait accompli:* "What's done is done. It can't be changed." Or a resort to company policy: "I can't do anything about it. It's company policy." Or a reference to a previous commitment: "I told the membership that I would resign as union negotiator before I would accept less than an eight percent raise." The other side may engage in endless foot-dragging and delay: "We'll get back to you." Or they may issue a final declaration: "You can take it or leave it!" Any other suggestion on your part is met with a no.

Attacks. Attacks are pressure tactics designed to intimidate you and make you feel so uncomfortable that you ultimately give in to the other side's demands. Perhaps the most common form of attack is to threaten you with dire consequences unless you accept their position: "Do it or *else!*" Your opponents may also attack your proposal ("Your figures are way out of line!"), your credibility ("You haven't been in this job long, have you?"), or your status and authority ("We want to talk to the *real* decision maker!"). Attackers will insult, badger, and bully until they get their way.

Tricks. Tricks are tactics that dupe you into giving in. They take advantage of the fact that you assume your counterpart is acting in good faith and is telling the truth. One kind of trick is manipulating the data—using false, phony, or confusing figures. Another is the "no authority" ploy, in which the other side misleads you into believing they have the authority to decide the issue, only to inform you after you have given up as much as you can that in fact someone else must decide. A third trick is the "add on," the last-minute additional demand that comes after your opponent has led you to believe you have already reached agreement.

Recognize the Tactic

The key to neutralizing a tactic's effect on you is to recognize it. If you recognize the other side's tactic as a stone wall, you are less likely to believe that they are inflexible. If you recognize an attack, you are less likely to fall prey to fear and discomfort. If you recognize a trick, you will not be taken in by the deception.

Consider an example. Mr. and Mrs. Albin had just sold their house—or at least that is what they thought they had done as they packed up all their belongings and prepared to move. Then the buyer, Mr. Maloney, demanded that the closing be postponed four months because he could not sell his own house. He refused to compensate the Albins for the delay. They in turn told him they would have to look for another buyer. Mr. Maloney responded, "You know, you're lucky you're dealing with someone like me. Other people I know would sue to prevent you from selling to anyone else. Your property could be tied up in court for years! But since we're practically friends by now, I'm sure we can avoid all that."

When Mr. Maloney left, Mr. Albin let out a sigh of relief and told his wife: "Thank God he's not going to sue. We would have been stuck in this place for years. Maybe we should accommodate him a little." Whereupon Mrs. Albin replied, "Honey, you've just been threatened in a nice way, and you don't even realize it. He *is* the type who'd sue, and we need to deal with him accordingly." Mr. Albin reacted to Mr. Maloney's tactic with fear—just as Mr. Maloney intended. In contrast, Mrs. Albin controlled her reaction by naming the game.

Many ploys depend on your not knowing what is being done to you. Suppose your customer tells you that he loves the deal but that his partner won't let him sign the contract without substantial changes. If you don't realize that he is using his partner as a "bad guy," you may agree innocently to the changes. Recognizing the tactic, however, puts you on your guard.

The hardest tactics to recognize are lies. You need to watch for *mismatch*—between their words, on the one hand, and their previous words or actions, facial expressions, body language, and tone of voice, on the other. Whereas liars can manipulate words, they cannot easily control the anxiety that raises their voice pitch. Nor can they control the symmetry of their facial expressions; a liar's smile, for instance, may become crooked. Bear in mind that anxiety can stem from other causes and that one clue alone is unreliable. You need to look for multiple clues.

Watching out for tactics means being alert, not overly suspicious. Sometimes you may have misunderstood the other person's behavior. One of the most celebrated political images in modern times is that of Soviet Premier Nikita Khrushchev pounding his shoe on the podium while delivering a speech at the United Nations in 1960. Everyone interpreted his histrionics as a tactic aimed at intimidating the West; a man who would pound his shoe one moment might use his nuclear weapons the next! Thirty years later, Khrushchev's son Sergei explained his father had had something far different in mind. Khrushchev, who had rarely been outside the Soviet Union, had heard that people in the West loved passionate political debate. So he gave his audience what he thought they wanted—he pounded his shoe to make his point. When people were shocked, no one was more surprised than Khrushchev himself. He had just been trying to look like one of the guys. What became the very image of the irrational Russian was apparently the result of a simple cross-cultural misunderstanding.

So put on your radar, not your armor. Make a mental note when you detect a possible trick or subtle attack. Neutralize it by naming it, and keep it in mind as a possibility, not a certainty. Look for additional evidence, remembering that difficult people rarely limit themselves to a single tactic.

Know Your Hot Buttons

To properly neutralize the effect of the other side's tactic on you, you need to recognize not only what they are doing but also what you're feeling.

The first clue that we are reacting usually comes from our bodies. Our stomachs get tied up in knots. Our hearts start to pound. Our faces flush. Our palms sweat. These are all visceral responses signaling that something is wrong and that we are losing our composure in the negotiation. They are cues that we need to go to the balcony.

Each of us has certain emotional susceptibilities, or "hot buttons." Some of us react bitterly to even minor criticism, or see red when we think someone is making fun of us. Some of us can't stand to have our ideas rejected. Others of us give in because we feel guilty, or because we are worried people won't like us, or because we don't want to cause a scene.

If you understand what your "hot buttons" are, you

can more easily recognize when your opponent is pushing them. Recognizing them in turn allows you to control your natural reaction. If you hate being called disorganized and you *know* you hate it, you can prepare yourself to deal with it. When someone calls you chaotic, you can simply shrug it off.

We live and work in competitive environments. So expect verbal attacks and don't take them personally. Remember that your accusers are hoping to play on your anger, fear, and guilt. They may want you to lose control of your emotions so that you cannot negotiate effectively. As children we learned when a playmate insulted us to say: "Sticks and stones may break my bones, but words will never hurt me." It is a simple lesson we would do well to remember as adults.

When you are being attacked, it may help to see your opponent as someone who doesn't know any better. Consider the approach taken by a woman whose boss periodically savaged her in front of her peers: "I was carrying him home in my head, driving myself and my family crazy. . . . But then I decided he wasn't my life. I began to detach myself and say, 'Poor guy, he doesn't know a better way to behave.' " No matter what he did, she wouldn't react: "He saw that he wasn't getting to me and his bullying behavior began to subside."

Buy Time to Think

Once you have named the game and forestalled your immediate reaction, the next step is to buy yourself time to think—time to go to the balcony.

Pause and Say Nothing

The simplest way to buy time to think in the middle of a tense negotiation is to pause and say nothing. It does you little good to respond when you're feeling angry or frustrated. Your judgment is distorted. This is not simply a psychological fact; it results from actual biochemical changes associated with anger and stress. Even taking a few seconds for these changes to dissipate will allow you to see things more objectively. Hence the wisdom of pausing before you reply. As Thomas Jefferson once put it: "When angry, count ten before you speak; if *very* angry, a hundred."

Pausing will not only give you a chance to step up to the balcony for a few seconds, but it may also help the other side cool down. By saying nothing you give them nothing to push against. Your silence may make them feel a little uncomfortable. The onus of keeping the conversation going shifts back to them. Uncertain about what is going on in your head, they may respond more reasonably. Some of the most effective negotiation is accomplished by saying nothing.

Suppose, however, that your opponent continues to rage. A movie producer, for instance, had a boss who used to blow up over the most trivial matters. The producer told a friend that he felt like punching his boss in the nose. The friend counseled, "Think about it this way. He's not yelling *at* you, he's yelling *for* himself. Next time he shouts at you, this is what you do. You lean back in your chair, fold your arms, and let his screams wash over you. Tell yourself how much good it's doing him to get it out of his system." The movie producer reported later that the plan worked wonders.

The same approach has been used to head off the ver-

bal battles that so often erupt in labor-management negotiations. In one case, both sides adopted a ground rule
that "only one person can get angry at a time." The other
side was obliged not to react; to do so would be an ad-
mission that they were weak and could not control themselves. The rule helped break the escalating cycle of action
and reaction.

You obviously can't eliminate your feelings, nor do you
need to do so. You need only to disconnect the automatic
link between emotion and action. Feel the anger, frustration, or fear—even imagine attacking your opponent if
you like—but *don't* channel your feelings and impulses into
action. Suspend your impulses; freeze your behavior.
While it may feel like hours, it will probably last only a few
seconds. This may not be easy when your opponent is
shouting or stonewalling, but it is necessary for successful
negotiation. Follow the biblical dictum: "Be quick to hear,
slow to speak, and slow to act."

Rewind the Tape

You can pause for only so long. To buy more time to think,
try rewinding the tape. Slow down the conversation by
playing it back. Tell your counterpart: "Let me just make
sure I understand what you're saying." Review the discussion up to that point.

Suppose you have just concluded a sale and you are
going over the contract with the customer. "I think we
have a terrific package here," he says, "and I'd be willing
to go ahead if you will throw in the service contract, you
know, gratis. What do you say? Can we call it a deal?" The
customer extends his hand.

If you react to the trick and decide yes or no on the

spot, there is a good chance you will make the wrong decision. To give yourself time on the balcony, rewind the tape. Look the customer in the eye and say, "Hold on, Larry. I'm not sure I'm following you. Let's back up for a minute and review how we got here. We started discussing this deal three months ago, back in March, right?"

"I guess so," Larry says.

"At the start I thought you said you wanted to negotiate the service contract separately from the purchase."

"Yes, but I've changed my mind on that."

"Larry, correct me if I'm wrong, but didn't you and I reach final agreement on all the clauses the day before yesterday?"

Whichever way Larry responds at this point, you are on the balcony, no longer reacting to his last-minute demand. You have not fallen for the trick. In fact, you have now caused Larry to shift from being on the offensive to being slightly on the defensive.

Tactics such as Larry's are like magic tricks; they are done so quickly you often don't see the sleight of hand. By rewinding the tape—which interrupts the routine and slows it down—you give yourself time to recognize the trick and neutralize its impact.

If the other side overloads you with information, hoping you will overlook a hidden drawback in their proposal, don't hesitate to say, "You've given me too much information to digest so quickly. Let's back up." Or "I need you to tell me again how the different components of your plan work together. I missed the connections between a couple of them." By asking the other side to give a detailed account, you can more easily spot the flaws in their logic.

An easy way to slow down the negotiation is to take careful notes. Writing down what your counterpart says gives you a good excuse: "I'm sorry, I missed that. Could you please repeat it?" Keeping a record not only buys you time to think, but also shows that you are taking the other person seriously.

Some people are afraid they will appear stupid if they say "I'm not sure I'm following you." Ironically, they are the ones most likely to be taken in, because they don't ask the questions they ought to ask. Successful negotiators learn that appearing a little obtuse can be a negotiating advantage. It allows you to slow down the discussion. You need not pretend to be stupid. Simply ask for some clarification: "I'm afraid I don't understand why you waited until now to ask for a discount."

If you can't think of anything else to say on the spot, you can always resort to the rote phrase, "Let me make sure I understand what you're saying."

Take a Time-out

If you need more time to think, you should take a break. Too many negotiations go on and on as each person reacts to the other's provocations. A time-out gives both sides a chance to cool off and go to the balcony. Negotiations are more productive when they are broken up by frequent time-outs.

You might be afraid that calling for a break will be interpreted as a sign of indecisiveness or weakness, as if you couldn't take the heat. The solution is to find a natural excuse. Such an excuse may be as simple as "We've been talking for some time now. Before continuing, let me suggest a quick coffee break." Or "That's a good question. Let me find out and get back to you right away." It helps to have a ready excuse.

One of the best excuses is to call a caucus with your

negotiating team. You might be worried about looking conspiratorial, but calling a caucus is perfectly legitimate; the other side may have just offered new information or made a new proposal, and you need a chance to discuss it among yourselves. If you are buying a car, tell the high-pressure salesperson, "My wife and I would like a moment to think about the decision. We're going to go for a walk around the block. We'll be back in half an hour." If you are negotiating by yourself, caucus on the phone with a colleague, boss, or friend.

If you can't leave the room, try to take a time-out from the negotiation by temporarily diverting the conversation with a story or joke. One union negotiator keeps snapshots of his fishing trips in his pocket and tosses them on the table when things get tense. All the participants start talking about their own adventures. When negotiations resume, tensions have abated.

Another way to take time out during the negotiation is to bring along a negotiating partner. That way you can spell each other; as one person talks, the other can go to the balcony and keep his eyes on the prize. Police negotiators dealing with a hostage-taker routinely work with a partner who gives them unbiased and realistic feedback on how they're doing, makes sure they don't become reactive, and relieves them when they get tired.

Don't Make Important Decisions on the Spot

In the presence of the other person, you are under strong psychological pressure to agree. One simple rule of thumb will help keep you out of trouble: Never make an important decision on the spot. Go to the balcony and make it there.

If the other side springs a contract on you and demands

an immediate signature, say: "My lawyer insists on check-
ing everything over. You know how lawyers are." Or ask:
"You've put a lot of time and thought into this, haven't
you?" As they nod agreement, continue, "In that case, I'd
like to do it justice by studying it carefully before responding." Fold up the document and put it away, saying: "I'll
get back to you tomorrow."

   While it is generally better to sleep on a prospective
decision, it isn't always possible. If an immediate response
is required, tell the other side: "I don't want to slow things
down. Let me make a quick phone call to my office, and
I'll get right back to you. If you'll excuse me, I'll make that
call right now." Even if you have time only to step out into
the corridor for a moment, it will help. Once you are away
from the table, the psychological pressure eases. It no
longer seems so urgent to reach a decision. Having suspended your initial reaction, you can now consider the
decision in a more objective fashion—on the balcony.

   Don't let yourself be hurried. If the other side sets a
deadline, don't hesitate to test it by adjourning the meeting.
If they are serious about the deadline, they will let you
know. Remember that agreement requires your assent.
Your worst enemy is your own quick reaction; only *you* can
make the concession you will later regret.

Don't Get Mad, Don't Get Even, Get What You Want

In sum, the most natural thing to do when faced with a
difficult person or situation is to react. It is also the biggest
mistake you can make.

The first thing you need to do in a negotiation is not to control the other person's behavior but to control your own. Suspend your natural reaction by naming the game. Then buy yourself time to think. Use the time to keep your eyes on the prize—an agreement that satisfies your interests, certainly better than your BATNA can. Instead of getting mad or getting even, concentrate on getting what you want. That is what going to the balcony is all about.

2

Don't Argue:

STEP TO THEIR SIDE

Rarely is it advisable to meet prejudices and passions
head on. Instead, it is best to appear to conform to them
in order to gain time to combat them. One must know
how to sail with a contrary wind and to tack until one
meets a wind in the right direction.

—*Fortune de Felice, 1778*

An AT&T sales team was negotiating to sell Boeing a new
telecommunications system valued at $150 million. The
sales team made a persuasive pitch on the kind of service
to be delivered, the company's prompt response to problems, and the speed of repairs.

Then the Boeing purchasing director said, "Fine. Now
put each one of your promises in writing. And we want
guarantees that if the system isn't fixed on time, you'll pay
us damages."

"We'll make our best efforts," replied the AT&T sales

chief, "but we can't be held liable for all the things that can go wrong. Lightning can strike—"

"You're fooling around with us!" interrupted the Boeing negotiator, losing his temper. "First you tell us about your services—now you're not willing to commit yourself to what you promised!"

"That's not true!" protested the sales chief, aghast at the turn in the negotiation. "Let me see if I can explain—"

But the Boeing negotiator refused to listen. "You're not negotiating in good faith!" he complained. "We can't deal with you."

The AT&T sales chief made a last-ditch effort: "Let's talk about it. Maybe we can put some of it in writing." But the Boeing purchasing director had already made up his mind. He and his team walked out the door.

What happened? When AT&T refused to go along with Boeing's demand, the Boeing negotiator got angry and went on the attack. The AT&T sales chief defended himself, but this just fueled the buyer's anger. When the sales chief tried to explain, the buyer wouldn't listen. Nothing seemed to work.

The mistake, a common one, is in trying to reason with a person who is not receptive. Your words will fall on deaf ears or be misconstrued. You are up against the barrier of emotion. The other side may feel distrustful, angry, or threatened. Convinced they are right and you are wrong, they may be unwilling to listen.

It is tempting to ignore the emotion and focus on the problem instead, but this is unlikely to work. The negative emotions will emerge in the form of inflexible positions. Before you can discuss the problem, you need to disarm the person. Going to the balcony has enabled you to regain your mental balance. Now you need to help the other side

regain theirs. Your challenge is to create a favorable climate in which you can negotiate.

Disarming the other side means defusing their hostile
emotions. It means getting them to hear your point of view.
And it means garnering a measure of their respect. They
don't need to like you, but they do need to take you seriously and treat you as a human being.

The secret of disarming is surprise. To disarm the other
side, you need to do the opposite of what they expect. If
they are stonewalling, they expect you to apply pressure;
if they are attacking, they expect you to resist. So don't
pressure; don't resist. Do the opposite: Step to their side.
It disorients them and opens them up to changing their
adversarial posture. Moreover, as practitioners of Japanese
martial arts have long recognized, it is hard to attack someone who is suddenly on your side. And most important,
it puts you and your opponent side by side—just where
you want to be in order to engage in problem-solving negotiation.

Stepping to their side means doing three things: listening, acknowledging, agreeing. Listen to what they have to
say. Acknowledge their point, their feelings, and their competence and status. And agree with them wherever you
can.

Stepping to their side may be the last thing you feel
like doing in a confrontational situation. When they close
their ears, you naturally feel like doing the same. When
they refuse to recognize your point of view, you certainly
don't feel like recognizing theirs. When they disagree with
everything you say, you may find it difficult to agree with
anything they say. Although entirely understandable, this
tit-for-tat response is a recipe for stalemate.

To break through the other side's resistance, you need
to reverse this dynamic. If you want them to listen to you,

begin by listening to them. If you want them to acknowledge your point, acknowledge theirs first. To get them to
agree with you, begin by agreeing with them.

Listen Actively

Too often negotiations proceed as follows: Party A sets
out their opening position. Party B is so focused on figuring out what they will say that they don't really listen.
When Party B's turn comes to lay out *their* position, Party
A thinks, "They didn't respond to what I said. They must
not have heard me. I'd better repeat it." Then Party B
concludes that they, too, have not been properly heard,
so they repeat their position. And on it goes—in a dialogue of the deaf. "Everything has been said before," says
a character in a novel by André Gide, "but since nobody
listens, we have to keep going back and beginning all
over again."

You have an opportunity to interrupt the chorus of
monologues if you are willing to be the first to listen.

Give the Other Side a Hearing

Listening to someone may be the cheapest concession you
can make. We all feel a deep need to be understood. By
satisfying that need, you can help turn the negotiation
around.

Consider a contract negotiation between union and
management at an Inland Steel container plant. The cor-

porate counsel took a rigid position on the crucial issue of wage arbitration, saying, "Now *that* is one I believe we're going to have to *insist* on." The general manager, Robert Novy, added, "That is putting it pretty mildly."

Normally the union would have counterattacked, management would have vehemently defended its position, and after a futile argument a strike would have ensued. Indeed, the previous breakdown in negotiations had resulted in a mutually disastrous 191-day strike, and everyone expected a strike this time too. But instead of counterattacking, chief union negotiator Jake Shafer said quietly, "I am interested in Mr. Novy's statement. You say, 'That is putting it pretty mildly.' "

With this invitation, Novy went on to explain at length why management felt so strongly about the issue. Having received the satisfaction of a full hearing, management in turn gave the union a hearing of *its* concerns. It may have seemed at the time like a small tactical move, but Shafer's decision to sit back and ask management to discuss its point of view broke open the deadlocked issue for eventual resolution. The strike that everyone expected never materialized.

Listening requires patience and self-discipline. Instead of reacting immediately or plotting your next step, you have to remain focused on what your counterpart is saying. Listening may not be an easy thing to do, but, as the story of Inland Steel demonstrates, it can be enormously valuable. It offers a window into the other side's thinking. It gives you a chance to engage them in a cooperative task— that of understanding *their* problem. And it makes them more willing to listen to you.

If the other side is angry or upset, the best thing you can offer is a full hearing of their grievance. Don't interrupt—even if you feel they are wrong or insulting. Let them know you're listening by maintaining eye contact, nodding occasionally, and responding with "uh-huh" or "I see." When they wind down, ask quietly if there is anything more they would like to add. Encourage them to tell you everything that is bothering them by using such phrases as "Yes, please go on" and "Then what happened?"

People derive genuine satisfaction from voicing their feelings and resentments. Customer-service managers know that even if there is little they can do to help an angry, dissatisfied customer, offering a full and respectful hearing can often be enough to keep the customer coming back.

Once you have heard the other side out, they will most likely become less reactive, more rational, and more responsive to problem-solving negotiation. It is no coincidence that *effective negotiators listen far more than they talk.*

Paraphrase and Ask for Corrections

It is not enough for you to listen to the other side. They need to know that you have *heard* what they have said. So reflect back what you hear. A conversation between a salesperson and an unhappy customer might go this way:

CUSTOMER: I bought this answering machine from you barely six months ago and now you can hardly hear the voices. It's not the tape—I replaced it. What kind of lousy machines do you sell here? I'm losing business because of you. I want it replaced right now with a quality machine or this won't be the last you hear of me.

SALESPERSON: Okay, let me make sure I understand. You bought this machine here six months ago to use in your business. But now you can't hear the voices. You need a working machine, and time is of the essence. Have I got it right?

CUSTOMER: That's right.
SALESPERSON: Let's see what we can do for you.

Paraphrasing means summing up your understanding of what the other side has said and repeating it back in your own words. Remember to retain *their* point of view. Adding your own or trying to make them see the error of their ways will not help. It will give the customer little satisfaction if you say "*You* couldn't make it work so you've brought it back?"

Paraphrasing gives the other side the feeling of being understood as well as the satisfaction of correcting you. It gives you a chance to check and see whether you have gotten their message. Paraphrasing is one of the most useful techniques in a negotiator's repertoire.

Acknowledge Their Point

After listening to the other side, the next step is to acknowledge their point. You may be reluctant to do this because of your strong disagreement. But by omitting this step you miss a critical opportunity. Every human being, no matter how impossible, has a deep need for recognition. By satisfying that need you can help create a climate for agreement.

Acknowledging the other person's point does *not* mean that you agree with it. It means that you accept it as one valid point of view among others. It sends the message "I can see how you see things." It is conveyed in phrases such as "You have a point there" or "I know exactly what you mean" or "I understand what you're saying."

The other side's mind is often like a cluttered attic, full of old resentments and angers, gripes and stories. To argue with them just keeps all this stuff alive. But if you acknowledge the validity of what they say, it begins to lose its emotional charge. In effect, the stuff begins to disappear from the attic. By letting them tell their side of the story *and* acknowledging it, you create psychological room for them to accept that there may be another side of the story.

One of the most powerful and surprising ways to acknowledge the other side's point is to preempt it. Take the words out of their mouth. Tell them: "If I were in your shoes, this is the way I'd see it." Former U.S. Defense Secretary Robert McNamara used this approach at a 1989 meeting of key American, Soviet, and Cuban participants in the 1962 Cuban missile crisis. Sensing that the Soviets and the Cubans were defensive about why their governments had decided to secretly install nuclear missiles in Cuba, he announced, "If *I* had been a Cuban or Soviet leader at the time, I would have concluded that the Americans intended to invade Cuba. From the evidence you had available to you, you were right to reach that conclusion. But I must tell you that we had no such intention." By preemptively acknowledging what the Soviets and Cubans were thinking, McNamara made them more receptive to hearing his viewpoint.

Acknowledge Their Feelings

Don't ignore the other side's emotions. Behind their attack often lies anger; behind their stonewalling often lies fear. Until you defuse their emotions, your reasonable arguments will fall on deaf ears.

Imagine that an employee storms into your office and rages, "I'm sick of being cheated! I just found out that

Dayle Turner gets two thousand dollars more a year for doing the same job that I do. I'm through!"

Trying to explain why Dayle earns more money, even if the reason is a good one, may only make your employee angrier. Instead, you must acknowledge his feelings first: "You think we're taking advantage of you. I can understand that. I'd probably feel angry too."

This is not the response your employee expects. By acknowledging his feelings, you have helped him calm down.

He then asks, "Why shouldn't I make every penny as much as Dayle does? I do the same work!"

By asking you a question, albeit an angry one, he shows that he is ready to hear your explanation. Now you can proceed to reason with him.

Like the employee, the other side often feels embattled and unappreciated. It is disarming to be met with an acknowledgment rather than an argument. Telling them "I appreciate how you feel" or "If I were in your shoes, I'd be just as angry" lets them know their message has been heard and appreciated. Showing that you understand *why* they feel as they do enhances your acknowledgment.

One word of caution: The other person will usually be able to tell whether or not your acknowledgment is sincere. Your intent, as expressed in your tone and body language, counts just as much as your words.

Offer an Apology

Perhaps the most powerful form of acknowledgment is an apology. This is a lesson we all learn as children. If you say the magic words "I'm sorry," you can continue playing the game. Unfortunately, it is a lesson we often forget as adults. Take the Columbia law professor who put the following question to his contracts class:

"Seller promises Buyer to deliver widgets at the rate of one thousand a month. The first two deliveries are perfect. However, in the third month Seller delivers only nine hundred and ninety widgets. Buyer becomes so incensed that he rejects deliveries and refuses to pay for the widgets already delivered. If you were Seller, what would you say?"

The professor was looking for a discussion of the various common-law theories that would, as he put it, "allow Seller to crush Buyer." He looked around the room for a volunteer, but found none. "As is so often the case with first-year students," he reported, "I found that they were all either writing in their notebooks or inspecting their shoes. There was, however, one eager face, that of an eight-year-old son of one of my students. He was in class because his mother couldn't find a sitter. Suddenly he raised his hand. Such behavior, even from an eight-year-old, must be rewarded.

" 'Okay,' I said, 'what would you say if you were the seller?'

" 'I'd say, "I'm sorry." ' "

As the child seemed to know instinctively, "crushing" an opponent is not the right answer. We often overlook the simple power of an apology. The buyer was outraged because he felt wronged. What such people most often want is the recognition that they *have* been wronged. Only when that acknowledgment has been made will they feel safe in negotiating. An apology thus creates the conditions for a constructive resolution of the dispute.

Your apology need not be meek, nor an act of self-blame. To a disgruntled customer, you could say, "I'm sorry you've had this problem. You're one of my favorite customers and the last person I'd want to see unhappy.

What can we do to make it up to you?" Even if the other side is primarily responsible for the mess you are in, consider apologizing for your share. Your bold gesture can set in motion a process of reconciliation in which they apologize for *their* share.

Project Confidence

You may be afraid that acknowledging the other side is an act of weakness. To the contrary, acknowledgment reflects your strength. To ensure that they recognize this, project confidence as you acknowledge them. In dealing with an attack, for example, put as reasonable an expression on your face as you can muster. Adopt a calm, confident posture and tone. Stand up straight, make eye contact, and use your attacker's name. Fearlessness disarms.

Consider how an American diplomat, held hostage in Iran from 1979 until 1981, took control by acknowledging his opponents. Whenever his guards came into his room, he would invite them to sit down. "They became *my* guests," explained the diplomat, "and in this small way, I established command of the situation. I created the unmistakable sense that this was *my* space, *my* territory, and it did wonders for my well-being."

Agree Wherever You Can

Once you have listened to the other side and acknowledged what they have said, the next step is to agree wherever you can. It will be hard for them to attack someone who agrees with them.

Agree Without Conceding

You don't need to concede a thing. Simply focus on issues on which you already agree. An American senator told his legislative staff, "Don't argue with my constituents, even if they're wrong. All you do is lose me votes. Do the *opposite* of what they taught you in graduate school. There, if someone said something you agreed with ninety-nine percent, you said, 'I disagree,' and you focused on the one percent of disagreement. Here, if my constituent says something you disagree with ninety-nine percent, I want you to say, 'I agree with you' and focus on the one percent of agreement." It is natural to focus on differences because differences cause the problem. At the outset, however, you are better off focusing on your common ground.

Look for any opportunity to agree—even if it is only in a humorous way. Humor has the added benefit of humanizing you in the other person's eyes. Consider the example of a fund-raiser for United Way who had to solicit contributions one day from a group of truck drivers as they showed up for work at six o'clock in the morning. At that hour no one had the slightest interest in United Way, but the boss had ordered the drivers to attend the meeting. As the fund-raiser was cheerily showing a videotape about the charity, the atmosphere in the room turned tense. When he passed out yellow pencils and pledge cards, the truck drivers stared at them and did nothing. Finally, one burly truck driver stood up, shook his pencil in a threatening fashion at the fund-raiser, and growled, "I'll tell you what you can do with this *pencil*!"

There was an awkward moment as everyone waited to see how the United Way representative would react. The fund-raiser looked the truck driver straight in the eye and said calmly, "Sir, I will be happy to do whatever you like with that pencil . . ." He paused, then added, " . . . *after* you sign the pledge card, of course." There was a brief moment of silence, and then one person started to laugh. Everyone joined in. The tension was broken. In the end, every truck driver signed a pledge card.

Accumulate Yeses

The key word in agreement is "yes." "Yes" is a magic word, a powerful tool for disarming the other side. Look for occasions when you can say yes to them without making a concession. "Yes, you have a point there." "Yes, I agree with you." Say yes as often as possible.

You should also try to *get* as many yeses as you can. One public speaker uses this technique effectively to handle hostile comments from the audience. If someone says, "Your proposal is utterly unrealistic," he responds, "Are you saying you don't see how my budget proposal can possibly erase the deficit within five years—is that what you mean?" The audience member says yes, and as he does, the relationship between the speaker and the critic changes. The "yes" transforms an antagonistic argument into the beginning of a reasoned dialogue.

Each yes you elicit from the other side further reduces tension. As you accumulate agreement, even if only on what they are saying, you create an atmosphere in which they are more likely to say yes to a substantive proposal.

Tune in to Their Wavelength

Agreement can be nonverbal too. If you observe two friends deep in conversation, you will often notice something peculiar. If one friend leans on an elbow, the other does too. If one speaks in a low voice, the other's voice gets lower too. Almost unconsciously they align themselves with each other in order to communicate more effectively. Each is sending the other a subtle message: "I am like you."

Much of the message comes across in the form, not the content, of the communication. Observe the other side's communicative manner. If they speak slowly, you may want to slow down your own speaking rate. If they talk softly, you may want to lower your voice. Observe their body posture too. If they lean forward to emphasize a point, consider leaning forward, too, to show your interest. Don't mimic. Just adapt your own communicative style to be more like theirs. Your goal is to tune in to the same wavelength.

It also pays to be sensitive to the other side's language. If they are speaking in a colloquial fashion, you may want to make your language more colloquial. If they are from a different culture, it helps to learn and use a few polite phrases from *their* language in order to show your interest and respect.

People also use different "sensory languages," depending on whether they process information primarily through their eyes, ears, or feelings. If the other side uses primarily visual terms such as "Can't you *see* what I'm saying?" or "Let's *focus* on that," try to match them with similar phrases: "I do *see* your point" or "I can *picture* what you're saying." If they use primarily auditory terms such as "*Listen* to this," respond with a phrase such as "I *hear* you." Or if their language is oriented around feelings, as in "That doesn't *feel* right to me," answer with phrases like, "I'm not *comfortable* either." Connect with your counterparts by using the language they understand best.

Acknowledge the Person

In listening to the other side, acknowledging their points, and agreeing whenever you can, you are in fact acknowledging them as people. You are showing them respect. Sometimes, however, you may want to acknowledge them in a more direct fashion.

Consider one of the world's most intractable disputes: the Arab-Israeli conflict. Until 1977, Arab leaders refused to recognize Israel's existence; they would not even call it by its name. Then, in November of that year, Egyptian President Anwar Sadat broke the taboo with his dramatic journey to Jerusalem. Nothing could have been more surprising to the Israelis, more confusing to their perceptions of the Egyptians, or more disarming than the arrival of an enemy leader in the country his army had attacked a mere four years earlier. With this one action, he broke through the psychological barrier that constituted, in his words, ninety percent of the conflict. He created a climate that eventually produced a peace treaty between Egypt and Israel, which few had thought possible.

By acknowledging the person, you create what psychologists call "cognitive dissonance," an inconsistency between perception and reality. The other side may think of you as an adversary. When you acknowledge them personally, you are acting as a friend or colleague, thus inducing them to change their perceptions of you in order to reduce the cognitive dissonance. Just as Sadat capitalized on the Israeli perception of him as a warmonger, you can capitalize on the other side's negative perception of you by acting in a way that shatters their stereotypes.

Reaffirming the person does not mean reaffirming the behavior. Parents continue to love their eight-year-old even after he puts glue between the newspaper pages and tries to strangle his younger sister. You need to distinguish between the person and the behavior.

Acknowledge Their Authority and Competence

Suppose you are trying to persuade a difficult boss to change his mind about an office issue. He may perceive you to be personally challenging his authority or competence. Are you implying, he wonders, that he is somehow incompetent or wrong? He will likely react by becoming even more resistant to what you have to say. To reassure him that you are not challenging him personally, you need to preface your remarks with a phrase such as "You're the boss" or "I respect your authority."

If the other person has a big or vulnerable ego, think of it as an opportunity rather than an obstacle. A person whose ego needs stroking is dependent on the recognition of others. To the extent you can satisfy this need for recognition, you can disarm the person. If you are seeking an exception to company policy from a self-important or insecure bureaucrat, you might begin by saying, "I've been told that you are the most knowledgeable person on this policy." To make your acknowledgment more credible, base it on facts. Instead of telling a departmental rival

"You're the best salesperson around"—which she may dismiss as mere flattery—you might say, "Your presentation to the board was succinct, persuasive, and to the point. I don't think I've ever seen it done better."

Build a Working Relationship

One of the best ways to acknowledge the other side is to build a working relationship. Invite them out for coffee or lunch, or meet for a drink after work. You can use such occasions to talk about hobbies and families, or whatever their interests are. Take time for small talk before the negotiation session begins and as it ends. Little gestures of goodwill can go a long way.

A good working relationship is like a savings account you can draw on in moments of trouble. When we deal with someone we know and like, we tend to attribute adverse events to extenuating circumstances: "Oh, I guess he didn't show up for the meeting because he was ill." When we deal with someone we don't like, we tend to attribute the same events to the person's basic nature: "He wants to keep me waiting to show me who has the upper hand." In short, if you have a positive relationship, your counterpart will be more inclined to give you the benefit of the doubt. You can thus prevent misunderstandings.

The best time to lay the foundation for a good relationship is *before* a problem arises. So if your job is likely to bring you into conflict with an individual, nurture the relationship from the earliest possible point. A production manager ought to have a healthy working relationship with his opposite number in marketing; a union chief, with her management counterpart; and a school principal, with the school board. When the other person is being difficult, you want to be able to say "Come on, Chris. We've always gotten on. We go back a long way."

Express Your Views—Without Provoking

Once you have heard and acknowledged the other side, they are far more likely to listen to you. Now is the time to get *your* views across. You need to do so, however, without making them close their ears.

The secret lies in changing your mind-set. The standard mind-set is *either/or:* Either you are right or the other side is. The alternative mind-set is *both/and.* They can be right in terms of their experience, and you can be right in terms of yours. You can say to them, "I can see why you feel the way you do. It's entirely reasonable in terms of the experience you've had. My experience, however, has been different." You can acknowledge their view and, without challenging it, express a contrary one. You can create an inclusive atmosphere in which differences can coexist peacefully while you try to reconcile them.

Don't Say "But," Say "Yes...And"

One of the most common methods of expressing your differences is to preface your views with the word "but." When your customer says "Your price is too high," you may be tempted to refute her statement with your own: "*But* this product is the highest quality you'll find!" Unfortunately, when your customer hears a "but," she may hear "I think you are wrong for the following reasons." Not surprisingly, she may stop listening.

The other side will be more receptive if you first acknowledge their views with a "yes" and then preface your own with an "and." After your customer complains about the high price, you could say, "*Yes*, you're absolutely correct that our price is higher. *And* what that increment buys you is higher quality, greater reliability, and better service!"

Even a direct disagreement can be framed inclusively: "I can see why you feel strongly about this, and I respect that. Let me tell you, however, how it looks from my angle," or "I am in total agreement with what you're trying to accomplish. What you may not have considered is..." Whatever language you use, the key is to present your views as an addition to, rather than a direct contradiction of, the other person's point of view.

Make "I" Statements, Not "You" Statements

As you express your views, you will be less likely to provoke the other side if you speak about yourself rather than about them. After all, your own experience is all you really know about anyway.

Suppose you are dealing with a difficult teenager who promised to come home by midnight but didn't show up until three o'clock in the morning. You could express your views by saying, "You broke your word! You're irresponsible." Or, "You only care about yourself. You never think about your family!" These are called "you"-statements. The teenager naturally becomes defensive and angry. He tunes out the familiar parental lecture.

Suppose that you were to say instead: "Ken, I felt let down last night. I worried myself sick that something terrible had happened to you. I even called the highway patrol to see if you had been in an accident." Instead of attacking, you express your feelings and experience. These are "I"-statements. The underlying message is the same, but phrased this way, your feelings are more likely to be heard.

The essence of an I-statement is to describe the impact of the problem on you. You are giving the other side information about the consequences of their behavior in a form that is hard for them to reject—because it is *your* experience. Common phrases to use are: "I feel...," "I get upset when...," "I'm not comfortable with...," and "The way I see it is..."

An I-statement does not challenge the other side's views but simply offers them a different perspective—yours. It does not tell them what to do or how to think or how to feel. They are entitled to their opinions, and you are entitled to yours.

Note that just putting an "I" in front of a you-statement does not make it an I-statement. Telling your teenager "I feel that you have been irresponsible" or "I feel that you broke your word" is still accusatory and provokes the same defensive reaction. An I-statement focuses on *your* needs, concerns, feelings, and desires, not the other person's shortcomings.

Stand Up for Yourself

Don't hesitate to stand up for yourself. When threatened by the truck driver, the United Way fund-raiser did more than just humorously acknowledge his demand. After saying "Sir, I would be happy to do whatever you like with that pencil," he added: "*after* you sign the pledge card, of course." He stood up for himself and his charity.

Standing up for yourself does not negate your acknowledgment. Acknowledgment from someone perceived as confident and strong is more powerful than acknowledgment from someone perceived as weak. The combination of seemingly opposite responses—acknowledging your counterpart's views *and* expressing your own—is more effective than either alone.

Consider the parents faced with a bawling five-year-old who does not want to be left at home with a baby-sitter. Should they give in and stay home? Should they threaten to spank the child or try to appease him? A leading child psychologist suggests a third strategy. With empathy, tell the crying child: "I know you wish we were not going out tonight. Sometimes when we are not here, you get scared. You wish we would stay with you, but your father and I are going to enjoy a dinner with friends tonight. We'll have dinner at home with you tomorrow." Acknowledge the other person's views *and* stand up for your own.

Acknowledge Your Differences with Optimism

Expressing agreement with the other side does not mean suppressing your differences. Indeed, it is often helpful to acknowledge them openly. It assures the other side that you have understood their perspective, which helps them relax. In many ethnic conflicts, for example, the parties only feel comfortable acknowledging areas of agreement *after* they have clearly delineated the areas of disagreement.

When you set out your differences, you may find they are not as great as either of you imagined. Sometimes, however, they seem overwhelming. So an optimistic stance on your part is critical. Affirm your interest in reaching agreement and assert your belief that a satisfactory solution is possible: "I think we *can* make a deal here." Be bold in acknowledging the other person's views, bold in asserting your own, and equally bold in expressing optimism that your differences can be resolved.

Create a Favorable Climate for Negotiation

In sum, the hurdles you face are the other side's suspicion and hostility, closed ears, and lack of respect. Your best strategy is to step to their side. It is harder to be hostile toward someone who hears you out and acknowledges what you say and how you feel. It is easier to listen to someone who has listened to you. And respect breeds respect.

Pleasantly surprised by your behavior, your opponent may think: "This person actually seems to understand and appreciate my problem. Since almost no one else does, that means this person must be intelligent." Then comes the clincher: "Maybe I can negotiate with this person after all." That is the crack in the wall you have been seeking.

To conclude, let's return to the negotiation between AT&T and Boeing described at the beginning of the chapter. Faced with the breakdown of the talks, the AT&T sales chief arranged a private meeting with the Boeing purchasing director. This is how he started off:

"I've been trying to understand your concerns. Correct me if I'm mistaken, but as you and your colleagues at Boeing see it, we've been misleading you, saying we're pre-

pared to give all this service but not to put it in writing
and be held liable for it. That seems to be bad-faith negotiating. So naturally you get angry and don't see the
point in continuing. Is that right?"

"That's right!" the Boeing buyer replied with fervor.
"How can we trust what you say? If *we* were negotiating
an aircraft sale and told the buyer the safety specifications
but then said we wouldn't put them in writing, the buyer
would walk right out the door. And he'd be right to leave.
If we won't be held accountable, we shouldn't be in the
airplane-building business. If *you* won't be bound by your
promises, you shouldn't be in the communications business!"

"You're absolutely right," acknowledged the AT&T
sales chief. "*I'd* feel the same way if I were you!"

Surprised, the Boeing negotiator asked, "Then *why*
won't you agree to put your promises in writing and agree
to pay damages if you don't live up to your commitment?"

The AT&T representative answered, "We will of
course put our promises in writing. Damages are an issue
we have trouble with but are at least willing to discuss. First
I want to see if I can clear up what's gotten us stuck. I
think I'm only beginning to understand it myself. I hear
you saying that Boeing has what you might call an 'engi-
neering culture.' There's no tolerance for ambiguity or
error when people's lives are at stake. So if you promise a
certain safety specification, you'd better be sure you're on
target. And, of course, everything has to be clearly speci-
fied in writing. Am I making sense?"

"Yes, what you're saying is right, but I don't see what
it has to do with our problem," said the Boeing buyer.

"If you'll bear with me, I'll try to explain why I think
it has everything to do with our problem. You see, at
AT&T we also have our engineers, but we're primarily in
the business of providing a service. We're more of a 're-

lationship culture.' We see our relationship with our clients as all-important—if the client's not happy, we're not happy. That's why people call us 'Ma Bell.' Now, when your mom tells you she's going to make your lunch and drive you to school, you don't say to her, 'Now, Mom, put it in writing and I'm going to hold you liable for damages,' do you?"

"Of course not."

"You just expect that she'll do the best she can. Now obviously there's a big difference between a household and a business, but this gives you a sense of where we're coming from. We make oral promises and fully expect to deliver on them. Our track record, you'll have to admit, is very good. It's a new experience for us to meet with a lot of skepticism and a demand for damages from a client. That's why we sort of collided with each other at the last meeting—you were coming from one place, which was absolutely right for you, and we were coming from another. Does this make any sense to you?"

"It's beginning to. Let me ask you . . . "

And so the negotiations got back under way.

How was the AT&T sales chief able to get the negotiation back on track? He preemptively acknowledged what he understood to be Boeing's concerns. He listened. He didn't try to refute his client's argument or defend AT&T. He simply acknowledged that the client was right. Once the Boeing negotiator's views were understood and appreciated, his anger subsided and he became more receptive. He asked a question, inviting the AT&T representative to offer his explanation. In short, the sales chief stepped first to the buyer's side. Only then did he describe how the situation looked from his side. In the end, he was able to allay his client's suspicions, get him to listen, and garner his respect. Not long afterward, AT&T and Boeing reached agreement on the $150 million sale.

3

Don't Reject:

REFRAME

Craft against vice I will apply.

—William Shakespeare,
Measure for Measure

Now that you have created a favorable climate for negotiation, the next challenge is to change the game. The
problem is that while you would like to discuss each side's
interests and how to satisfy them, the other side is likely to
insist on their *position*. While you may be flexible, they may
stonewall. While you may be attacking the problem, they
may be attacking you. Consider the following negotiation:

BUDGET DIRECTOR: I won't accept anything less than a ten per-
cent cut in your budget. So let's get to it, okay?
MARKETING CHIEF: That's impossible. We can't survive on that.
BUDGET DIRECTOR: I'm sorry, but I've already told the other

department heads you'll take the cut. If you don't, all the other deals will unravel.

MARKETING CHIEF: I understand your problem, but try to understand mine. I've just instituted a new plan in my department that will bring about greater productivity and substantial cost savings—but I can't implement it with a ten percent cut. Can't we cooperate and try to arrive at a solution that's good for the company?

BUDGET DIRECTOR: That's what I want—your cooperation. Let me put you down for that cut. Deal?

MARKETING CHIEF: I'm sorry, but I just can't agree to that.

BUDGET DIRECTOR: Look, I don't want to get you into any trouble. But I need that budget cut now.

MARKETING CHIEF: Suppose we take a six percent cut. That goes a long way toward meeting your target. How about that?

BUDGET DIRECTOR: Well, that makes it easier. Now you've only got to find four percent more.

MARKETING CHIEF: Six percent is as high as I can go.

BUDGET DIRECTOR: The president is going to hear about this!

What can you do if the other person takes an inflexible position? What if the person digs in ("I won't accept anything less than ten percent"), threatens ("I don't want to get you into any trouble"), or presents you with a *fait accompli* ("I've already told the other department heads that you'll take the cut")?

Since the other side's demand seems unreasonable, your natural temptation is to reject it out of hand. You respond to their position by advancing your own. They, of course, reject your position and reassert theirs. Even if you come back with a reasonable compromise, they may interpret it as your fallback position, pocket the concession, and press you for more. Before you know it, you are once again playing their game of hardball—precisely what you wanted to avoid.

Is there any way to draw them into *your* game of problem-solving negotiation?

To Change the Game, Change the Frame

Remember the batting secret of the great home-run hitter, Sadahara Oh. Oh looked on the opposing pitcher as his *partner*, who with every pitch was serving up an *opportunity* for him to hit a home run. Oh changed the game by *reframing* the situation.

To change the negotiation game, you need to do the same thing. Do the opposite of what you may feel tempted to do. Treat your opponent like a partner. Instead of rejecting what your opponent says, accept it—and reframe it as an opportunity to talk about the problem.

Reframing means redirecting the other side's attention away from positions and toward the task of identifying interests, inventing creative options, and discussing fair standards for selecting an option. Just as you might put a new frame around an old picture, you put a problem-solving frame around the other side's positional statements. Instead of rejecting their hard-line position, you treat it as an informative contribution to the discussion. Reframe it by saying, "That's interesting. *Why* do you want that? Help me understand the problem you are trying to solve." The moment they answer, the focus of the conversation shifts from positions to interests. You have just changed the game.

Consider the following example: In 1979, the SALT II arms-control treaty was up for ratification in the U.S. Senate. To obtain the necessary two-thirds majority, the Senate leaders wanted to add an amendment, but this required Soviet assent. A young U.S. senator, Joseph R. Biden, Jr., was about to travel to Moscow, so the Senate leadership asked him to raise the question with Soviet Foreign Minister Andrei Gromyko.

The match in Moscow was uneven: a junior senator head to head with a hard-nosed diplomat of vast experience. Gromyko began the discussion with an eloquent hour-long disquisition on how the Soviets had always played catch-up to the Americans in the arms race. He concluded with a forceful argument for why SALT II actually favored the Americans and why, therefore, the Senate should ratify the treaty unchanged. Gromyko's position on the proposed amendment was an unequivocal *nyet*.

Then it was Biden's turn. Instead of arguing with Gromyko and taking a counterposition, he slowly and gravely said, "Mr. Gromyko, you make a very persuasive case. I agree with much of what you've said. When I go back to my colleagues in the Senate, however, and report what you've just told me, some of them—like Senator Goldwater or Senator Helms—will not be persuaded, and I'm afraid their concerns will carry weight with others." Biden went on to explain their worries. "You have more experience in these arms-control matters than anyone else alive. How would *you* advise me to respond to my colleagues' concerns?"

Gromyko could not resist the temptation to offer advice to the inexperienced young American. He started coaching him on what he should tell the skeptical senators. One by one, Biden raised the arguments that would need to be dealt with, and Gromyko grappled with each of them. In the end, appreciating perhaps for the first time how the amendment would help win wavering votes, Gromyko reversed himself and gave his consent.

Instead of *rejecting* Gromyko's position, which would have led to an argument over positions, Biden acted as if Gromyko were interested in problem-solving and asked for his advice. He *reframed* the conversation as a constructive discussion about how to meet the senators' concerns and win ratification of the treaty.

Reframing works because every message is subject to interpretation. You have the *power of positive perception*, the ability to put a problem-solving frame around whatever the other side says. They will often go along with your reinterpretation, just as Gromyko did, partly because they are surprised that you have not rejected their position and partly because they are eager to pursue their argument.

Because they are concentrating on the *outcome* of the negotiation, they may not even be aware that you have subtly changed the *process*. Instead of focusing on competing positions, you are figuring out how best to satisfy each side's interests. You don't need to ask the other side's permission. Just start to play the new game.

Reframing is one of the greatest powers you have as a negotiator. *The way to change the game is to change the frame.*

Ask Problem-Solving Questions

The most obvious way to direct the other side's attention toward the problem is to tell them about it. But making assertions can easily arouse their resistance. The better approach is to ask questions. Instead of giving the other side the right answer, try to ask the right question. Instead of trying to teach them yourself, *let the problem be their teacher.*

The single most valuable tool in reframing is the problem-solving question. A problem-solving question focuses attention on the interests of each side, the options for satisfying them, and the standards of fairness for resolving differences. Here are some of the most useful questions:

Ask "Why?"

Instead of treating the other side's position as an obstacle, treat it as an opportunity. When they tell you their position, they are giving you valuable information about what they want. Invite them to tell you more by asking, "Why is it that you want that?" "What is the problem?" or "What are your concerns?" Find out what really motivates them.

How you ask something is just as important as *what* you ask. If direct questions sound confrontational, put them in an indirect form: "I'm not sure I understand why you want that," "Help me to see why this is important to you," or "You seem to feel pretty strongly about this—I'd be interested in understanding why." It helps to preface your question with an acknowledgment: "I hear what you're saying. I'm sure the company policy has a good purpose—could you please explain it to me?" In showing your interest and respect, remember that your tone, facial expressions, and body language are just as important as your words.

Asking questions to uncover interests is like peeling the layers of an onion. You uncover one layer after another, as in the following conversation:

"Why do you want to leave the job?" asked the senior partner in a New York law firm.

"Because I need more money and you can't give me enough of a raise," replied the young associate.

"What's the problem?"

"Well, my wife and I just had another child, and we need to move into a larger apartment."

"So what's the problem?"

"We can't find one that's rent-controlled."

Once the senior partner had gotten to the bottom of

the problem, he used his network to find the associate an apartment that fit the bill. The associate ended up staying with the firm for thirty more years, becoming a senior partner himself. Persistent probing of underlying interests helped produce a mutually satisfying agreement.

Don't forget the interests of the other side's constituents. The other side's hard-line position may have less to do with their own concerns than with those of their boss, board of directors, stockholders, union members, or family. Ask about *their* interests too.

Ask "Why Not?"

If the other side is reluctant to reveal their interests, take an indirect tack. If asking *why* doesn't work, try asking *why not*. Propose an option and ask "Why not do it this way?" or "What would be wrong with this approach?" People reluctant to disclose their concerns usually love to criticize. If you are immersed in a budget negotiation and ask "Why shouldn't we cut the budget for marketing?" the marketing chief may well answer, "I'll tell you why. Sales will plunge, the board will start breathing down our necks, and I'll end up typing up a new résumé." Without being aware of it, she has just given you valuable information about her interests—her concerns about sales, her worries about pressure from the board, and her fear of losing her job.

If the other side still won't reveal their interests, bring them up yourself and ask them to correct you. If you are trying to persuade a reluctant manufacturer to speed up production, you could say to him, "If I understand what you're saying, your interests are in keeping costs down, quality high, and the service reliable. Is that right?" Few people can resist the temptation to correct someone's misunderstanding of their interests. The manufacturer may reply, "That's not exactly right. You've forgotten about..." and off he goes telling you about his interests.

If the other side still resists, it may be because they fear you will use the information to take advantage of them. To build trust and set them at ease, tell them your interests first: "I'd like to speed up production in order to take advantage of the new market. My distributors are breathing down my neck for the product, and personally, I feel my credibility is on the line. Can you tell me a little about the constraints that make it hard for you to speed up production?" If revealing your interests makes you feel vulnerable, you don't need to tell all at the start. Give the other side a little information about your interests, ask them about theirs, then give them more information, and so on. Build trust incrementally.

Ask "What If?"

The next step is to engage the other side in discussing options. To introduce a host of possible solutions *without* challenging their position, use one of the most powerful phrases in the English language: "What if?"

Suppose your customer announces, "That's all the money we have in the budget to pay for this consulting project. We can't pay a penny more!" Ask, "*What if* we were to stretch out the project so that the excess could go into next year's budget?" Or "*What if* we were to reduce the magnitude of the project to fit within your budget constraints?" Or "*What if* we can help you show your boss how the benefits to your company justify asking for a budget increase?" If you can get your customer to address any one of these questions, you will have succeeded in changing the game. Suddenly you are exploring options together.

Turn the conversation into a brainstorming session. Take your counterpart's position and reframe it as one possible option among many. Suppose, for instance, you are having a difficult family negotiation about where to spend the Christmas holidays. Your spouse insists on going to his or her family's home. Instead of rejecting the proposal, you could say, "That's one possibility." Propose an option or two yourself and invite your spouse to suggest others: "Another possibility, of course, would be to spend it with my family. Or what if we divide it between the two— Christmas with yours and New Year's with mine? Got any other ideas?"

If your counterpart begins to criticize your options, you might say, "I'd like to hear your criticism, but can we put it off until we have all the options on the table? Then we can see which works best." Since judging inhibits creativity, invent first and evaluate later.

Ask for Their Advice

Another way to engage the other side in a discussion of options is to ask for their advice. It is probably the last thing they expect you to do. Ask "What would you suggest that I do?" "What would you do if you were in my shoes?" Or "What would you say to my constituents?" This is the approach Senator Biden took with Minister Gromyko.

It is flattering to be asked for advice. You are, in effect, acknowledging the other side's competence and status. It not only disarms them, but it also gives you a chance to educate them about your problem and the constraints facing you.

Imagine you have to get approval for an exception to company policy from a rigid bureaucrat. You anticipate that if you ask him directly, he will complain loudly about you and all the others who are trying to bend the rules. So instead you say, "Mr. Talbot, you have been recommended to me as an expert on company policy. I have a problem on which I would like to seek your advice." After explaining the situation, you ask, "How would you suggest that I proceed?"

Once the other side gets involved in your problem, they begin to develop a stake in living up to the positive and powerful role in which you have cast them. Often they will come up with a solution to your problem; Mr. Talbot may grant an exception to the policy.

If, however, he responds by reasserting the policy, acknowledge his concerns and continue to ask for his advice: "I recognize the reasons for this policy. It's important that you uphold it. Still, this project is very important for the company's future. How would you suggest we get it accomplished?" If Mr. Talbot says there is nothing *he* can do, then say, "I understand. Could you advise me about who could grant an exception?"

Asking for advice is one of the most effective ways you can change the game.

Ask "What Makes That Fair?"

The other side's position may strike you as unreasonable. Instead of rejecting it, however, you can use it as a jumping-off point for a discussion of standards of fairness. Act as if they must believe their position is fair—they usually do. Tell them: "You must have good reasons for thinking that's a fair solution. I'd like to hear them."

Suppose, for example, an important client expects free service to be thrown in with the price of the product. You may feel you can't say no without offending. Yet if you say yes, it will be an expensive decision. So you ask, "What's your thinking about what makes that fair? Does our competition throw in the service for free?" You are using a standard of fairness—in this case, market practice—so that your customer can see that the demand is unfair. As the French philosopher Blaise Pascal wrote more than three centuries ago: "People are usually more convinced by reasons they discovered by themselves than by those found by others."

In one acquisitions negotiation, the seller asked what seemed an excessively high price for the company. Instead of rejecting the price, the buyer set out to educate him. He began by asking what profits the seller expected his company to make in the first year. The seller answered, "We will do four million this year, and that equals four hundred thousand in profits." Once the buyer had this optimistic point of reference, he was able to say, "I'm sure you'll meet that goal if you say you will. After all, you're running a hell of a ship here. But the price of that ship is based on your estimate. You know better than I the number of things that can throw that off. If you don't meet that projection, do we get a reduction in price?" By probing for the rationale behind the price, the buyer was able to win a considerable reduction without ever rejecting the price flat out.

Sometimes, to start a discussion about a fair outcome, you may need to propose a standard yourself. In the acquisitions negotiation the buyer suggested using standard accounting practice to determine a fair price. He told the seller: "My accountant has brought up a point, though I'm sure it's something you're already aware of. We're probably going to have to set up a receivables reserve of about half a million dollars. . . . It's a sound accounting practice, considering the way your company looks. This could bring down the company's net worth and will mean we have to take a much harder look at the price tag you've put on it." The seller again lowered his price substantially.

If the other side rejects your standard, challenge them to come up with a better one. A discussion of different standards will still achieve your objective of shifting the focus from positions to fair outcomes.

Make Your Questions Open-Ended

Not just any question will do. A problem-solving question needs to be open-ended and eye-opening.

How you phrase the question determines the answer. When a company or government official says, "You can't do that; it's against our policy," you may be tempted to ask, "Can't the policy be changed?" And the answer you will undoubtedly receive is a resounding no. If you had thought about it beforehand, you might have anticipated the answer. In effect, your question set you up for a no.

Your counterpart can easily answer no to questions prefaced by "is," "isn't," "can," or "can't." So ask a question that cannot be answered by no. In other words, make it open-ended. Preface your question with "how," "why," "why not," "what," or "who." Your counterpart cannot easily answer no to questions such as "What's the purpose of this policy?" "Who has the authority to grant an exception?" and "How would you advise me to proceed?"

Too often people ask questions for which the other side has a ready-made response. Consider the example of a British arms-control negotiator who, no matter what he proposed to his Soviet counterpart, always received the

same monosyllabic answer: *"Nyet."* After a year of this treatment, the Briton took the Soviet aside and expressed his
exasperation. The Soviet negotiator replied, "It is *just*
as frustrating for me to negotiate with such inflexible instructions from Moscow. The problem is that you're always asking me questions for which I have instructions.
Why don't you ask me questions for which I have *no* instructions?" Puzzled, the British diplomat nevertheless
complied at their next negotiating session, posing a new,
eye-opening question. The Soviet negotiator thanked him
politely and told him that since he had no instructions on
how to answer, he would have to return to Moscow. There,
he was able to persuade his Kremlin superiors to give him
the flexibility needed to reach agreement.

Taking a cue from the two diplomats, you need to ask
questions for which the other side has no "instructions,"
no pat answer. Your questions should make them think—
just as Biden's queries compelled Gromyko to contend with
the senators' reservations. In considering your questions,
the other side may change their thinking and become more
amenable to agreement.

Tap the Power of Silence

Only half the power of a problem-solving question lies in
the question itself. The other half can be found in the
pregnant silence that follows as the other side struggles
with the question and mulls over their answer. A common
mistake is to deprive them of this creative time. If they do
not respond, you may feel a growing discomfort from the
silence. In normal conversation, when you see that your
question has made your companion uncomfortable, you
let him or her off the hook by breaking the silence.

You should resist this temptation and wait for an answer from your negotiating counterpart. After all, you have asked a perfectly legitimate question. Let the silence and discomfort do their work. The other side may eventually respond with information about their interests, or a possible option, or a relevant standard. The moment they do, they are engaged in the game of problem-solving negotiation.

Remember, it takes only one answer to get you going. So be persistent. If one question doesn't yield the results you are seeking, try another angle, just as a skillful interviewer would. If you observe the practice of successful negotiators, you will find that they ask countless questions.

Reframe Tactics

Problem-solving questions enable you to reframe the other side's *position* in terms of interests, options, and standards. But you also need to deal with their *tactics*, the stone walls, attacks, and tricks they use to get you to give in. How do you reframe their tactics so as to direct their attention toward the problem?

Go Around Stone Walls

What if your opponent takes an extreme position, tells you "Take it or leave it," or sets a rigid deadline? To go around a stone wall, you can ignore it, reinterpret it, or test it.

Ignore the stone wall. If the other side declares "Take it or leave it!" or "You have until five o'clock, or the deal is off!" you cannot be sure whether they mean it or are just bluffing. So test their seriousness by ignoring the tactic. Keep talking about the problem as if you didn't hear what they said, or change the subject altogether. If they are serious, they will repeat their message.

Reinterpret the stone wall as an aspiration. Suppose a union leader announces to you: "I've told my people that if I don't come back with a fifteen percent raise, they can have my head on a silver platter." He has locked himself in. If you challenge his commitment, you will only make it harder for him to back away. Instead, reinterpret his commitment as an aspiration and direct attention back to the problem: "We all have our aspirations, I guess. Management is under pressure from the downturn in the economy and would love to cut wages. But I think we'll both be better off being realistic and taking a hard look at the merits of the pay issue. What are other companies paying their workers for the same job?" Your reinterpretation makes it easier for him to make a graceful exit from his commitment.

Or imagine you have to deal with a rigid deadline laid down by your opponent. Instead of rejecting it, you can soften it by reinterpreting it as a target: "We would all like to conclude this negotiation by then. That would be ideal. We'd better get to work immediately." Then turn to the problem with great gusto to show your goodwill.

Take the stone wall seriously, but test it. A third approach is to test the stone wall to see if it's real. For instance, treat your opponent's deadline seriously, but as it approaches, arrange to be called away for an urgent phone call or meeting. Hostage negotiators, for example, will find some credible but "uncontrollable" event, such as a bank holiday, that makes it impossible for them to assemble the ransom money in time to meet the terrorists' deadline. One leading negotiator explains, "We like deadlines. The shorter, the better. Because once you've broken the deadline, you've knocked them off their game plan."

Another way to test a stone wall without directly challenging it is to ask questions. If a car salesperson declares that the price is final, you can ask whether you could get financing or a good trade for your old car. If the salesperson begins to show flexibility, you will have determined that the price may not in fact be final.

Don't forget that you can sometimes turn the other side's stone wall to your advantage. If they have given you an inflexible deadline, for example, you can say, "I'd like to be able to convene the board to make you a more generous offer, but *in view of the time problem*, this is the best I can do at the moment." Or "To meet *your* deadline, we'll need your help. Can you take care of pick-up and delivery?"

Deflect Attacks

What if your opponent threatens you, insults you, or blames you for something that has gone wrong? How can you reframe an attack, shifting the focus away from you toward the problem?

Ignore the attack. One approach is to pretend you didn't hear the attack and go on talking about the problem. Suppose you're a union leader dealing with a difficult boss who threatens to fire half the work force unless you give in to his demand for wage cuts. Drawing attention to the threat would just make it harder for him to back away. Replying "Don't be ridiculous. You'd never do it!" may only spur him on to prove he meant what he said. Instead, you should ignore the threat and focus on the company's financial plight: "I know you're under pressure to make your numbers look better. Tell me a little about our situation."

If the other side sees that their abusive tactics do not work, they will often stop. Take the buyer who liked to keep his vendors waiting outside his office in order to unsettle them and make them more pliable on the terms of the deal. One vendor decided to ignore the tactic, bringing a novel along to read. When the buyer finally ushered her in, the vendor made a show of reluctantly closing the book, as if she had not been inconvenienced in the slightest. When the buyer took a long phone call in the middle of the meeting, out came the novel. After two or three such meetings, the buyer realized the tactic wasn't working and stopped using it.

Reframe an attack on you as an attack on the problem. A second approach is to reinterpret the attack. Suppose you are trying to win departmental approval for a new product, and a co-worker takes you to task: "Don't you know any better than to submit a proposal that will never fly?" You could become defensive and hostile. *Or* you could ignore the personal criticism, acknowledge the point, and reinterpret it as an attack on the problem: "You may have a point there. How would you improve the proposal to make it fly?"

Your attacker is making two claims: first, that your proposal is no good; and second, that *you* are no good. You have the power to choose which claim you want to address.

By choosing the more legitimate concern about the proposal, you can effectively sidestep the personal attack and direct your opponent's attention toward the problem.

Reframe a personal attack as friendly. Another way of reframing a personal attack is to misinterpret it as friendly. Take the eighteenth-century general who had fallen into disfavor with the great Prussian warrior king, Frederick the Great. Coming upon the king, the general saluted him with the greatest respect, but Frederick turned his back. "I am happy to see that Your Majesty is no longer angry with me," murmured the general. "How so?" demanded Frederick. "Because Your Majesty has never in his life turned his back on an enemy," replied the general. Disarmed, Frederick took the general back into his favor.

In everyday life you can reframe a personal attack as a show of concern and shift the focus back to the problem. For example, if your opponent tries to unsettle you by saying "You know, you don't look too good. You sure you feel all right?" you could answer, "Thanks for your concern. I feel great now that we're getting close to agreement."

Reframe from past wrongs to future remedies. Your opponent's attack often takes the form of blame. In a discussion of the household budget, a husband accuses his wife: "You waste money on useless knickknacks! Remember that seventy-five-dollar ceramic cat you bought?" The wife retorts, "Well, what about you, Mr. Showboat, taking all your pals out for drinks last week? How much did *that* cost?" And on they go for hours, sniping about the past. The budget is forgotten.

The opportunity always exists to reframe the issue from the past to the future, from who was wrong to what can be done about the problem. The wife can say to her husband: "Yes, Ben, we both agreed it was too much to pay for the ceramic cat. I won't make the same mistake again. Now what about next month's budget? How do we make sure we keep to it?" When your opponent criticizes you for a past incident, don't miss the opportunity to ask "How do we make sure it never happens again?" Reframe the blame as joint responsibility for tackling the problem.

Reframe from "you" and "me" to "we." When husband and wife are quarreling about their budget, all you hear is *"You* did this!" and *"I* did not!" A simple change in language from "you" and "me" to "we" can help. The wife asks, "How do *we* make sure *we* stay within the budget?" "We" creates a side-by-side stance, drawing attention to common interests and shared goals.

A simple and powerful way to reframe the situation from "you" or "me" to "we" is through body language. When people argue, they usually stand or sit face-to-face, physically expressing their confrontation. So find a natural excuse to sit side by side. Pull out a document or proposed agreement and sit down next to your counterpart to review it. Or sit next to your spouse on the sofa instead of shouting across the kitchen counter. Talking side by side will not magically transform the situation, but it will reinforce the idea that you are partners facing a tough challenge together.

Expose Tricks

The toughest tactic to reframe is a trick. Tricks take advantage of common assumptions made in good-faith negotiation—that the other side is telling the truth, that they will deliver on their promises, that they do have the authority they imply, and that once an issue is resolved, it won't be renegotiated. Tricks are hard to reframe because they are already couched in the language of cooperation and reasonableness in order to deceive you.

You could, of course, challenge the trick directly, but the risks are high. For one thing, you might be mistaken. And even if you are right, your opponent is likely to take offense at being called a cheat or liar, and your relationship will suffer.

The alternative to rejecting the trick is to play along with it. Respond *as if* the other side were negotiating in good faith, but act a little slow and ask probing questions in order to test their sincerity. In other words, *play dumb like a fox*. If the other side is sincere, your questions will do no harm. If they are trying to deceive you, you will expose the trick. Since you have not confronted them, they can save face by pretending it was all a mistake or a misunderstanding.

Ask clarifying questions. Ask questions to check and clarify the other side's assertions. If you are purchasing a company and the seller has included outstanding accounts receivable in the company's net worth, say in a nonjudgmental tone, "You must have good reasons for believing that these accounts receivable will in fact be paid. I'd be interested in knowing why you think so." Check their assumptions when they quote "infallible" authorities or methodologies such as computers and spreadsheets. Don't hesitate to press a little. And watch for ambiguities in their answers as well as outright evasions. If you spot a contradiction, don't challenge it directly. Just act confused: "I'm sorry, I'm afraid I don't understand. Could you explain how this relates to what you said before?"

One way to test your suspicions is to ask the other side questions to which you already know the answers. You can learn a lot from observing how they shade their responses.

A common trick is to mislead you into believing that they have decision-making authority when they don't. You may use up all your flexibility only to discover that they have to get the approval of their boss or board, who may well ask for additional concessions. To protect yourself, ask questions early on to clarify the other side's authority: "Am I correct in assuming you have the authority to settle this matter?" Make sure you get a specific answer. If they don't have full authority, find out who else must agree and how long it will take to get the answer.

Another common trick is the last-minute demand *after* you have reached agreement. Instead of challenging the demand, you can ask, "Are you suggesting that we reopen the negotiation?" If your opponent says no, you can say, "Well then, I think we should just stick with the agreement we've already reached." If, however, the answer is yes, you can say, "All right. We'll treat it as a joint draft to which neither side is committed. You check with your boss, and I'll check with mine, and let's meet tomorrow to discuss possible changes." If your opponent gets something extra, you should get something in return.

Make a reasonable request. You have one advantage in dealing with tricksters that you don't have with people who are openly uncooperative, and that is their stake in appearing reasonable. So take them at their word and put it to the test, thereby placing them in a dilemma. Either they live up to their pretense of cooperation or they drop the sham altogether. In other words, you can administer a "reasonable request test."

Design a reasonable request that the other side would

agree to if they were genuinely cooperative. If, for instance, you suspect they might be concealing debts that are difficult to collect, say "If you don't mind, I'd like to have my accountant look over your books and check the accounts receivable, just as a standard business routine." If the seller refuses to let your accountant go over their books, they will look uncooperative, and you can conclude that you can't rely on what they have told you.

If your opponent cites a "hard-hearted partner" as justification for an additional demand, you can make the following request: "Excuse me, Jerry. I'm not sure I understand. Did we make a mistake in not including your bankers in our previous discussions? I hate to think that I've put you on the spot here. Maybe I should get together with them and go over the terms we discussed. Can you arrange a meeting?"

Jerry now has a choice. He can let you meet with the bankers—which should give you a better sense of their objections and whether this is indeed a trick. Or he can refuse to let you meet with them—which should put you on your guard. Or he can drop the tactic altogether and stick to the original agreement. Whatever the outcome, you are free to follow up with further reasonable requests and clarifying questions.

Turn the trick to your advantage. If you see through your opponent's trick, you can often turn it to your advantage. Suppose you are representing the wife in a divorce case. The husband promises to pay child support, but you have reason to believe he will fail to do so. When you raise your concern, his lawyer protests that the husband will certainly pay.

"Are you certain?" you ask.

"Absolutely, my client is an honorable man," replies his lawyer.

"Then he will surely not object to adding a clause that in the case of three months' nonpayment, my client will receive his equity in the house in substitution for child support."

The more vigorously the lawyer has affirmed the husband's reliability, the harder it will be to object.

Negotiate About the Rules of the Game

If, despite all your efforts, your opponent continues to resort to stone walls, attacks, and tricks, you need to reframe the conversation in yet another way. Recast it as a negotiation *about* the negotiation.

There are actually two "negotiations" going on. One is the negotiation about *substance:* the terms and conditions, dollars and cents. The second is the negotiation about the *rules of the game*. How is the negotiation to be conducted? If you watch parents and children, for instance, negotiating over everyday issues such as bedtime, you will observe that they are also constantly renegotiating the extent to which temper tantrums, threats, and bribes are acceptable tactics.

Usually this second negotiation remains tacit. If you haven't been successful in changing the game, however, you need to make this negotiation explicit. You need to talk about your opponent's behavior. Often it is sufficient simply to bring it up.

Bring It Up

People who use tactics are usually probing to see exactly what they can get away with. In order to get them to stop, you may need to *let them know you know* what they are doing. Bringing up their tactic sends the message "I wasn't born yesterday. I know the game you're playing. Your tactic isn't going to work." If they want an agreement, they will drop the tactic, because using it will only make agreement more difficult to reach.

The problem is that the other side may mistake your calling attention to their tactic as an attack. The secret is to reframe their tactic as an interesting contribution rather than as an underhanded trick.

Consider an example. Liz and Pam are two young lawyers trying to buy a set of used labor-law books from two established attorneys, Bob and Charlie. At the outset of the discussion, Bob announces in a firm voice, "The very least we'll accept for these books is $13,000. You can take it or leave it." Charlie, however, argues with his partner Bob: "Come on, these two are just starting out. Surely we can give them a break. How about calling it $11,000 and leaving it at that?" A fair market price for the books would be $7,000, but Bob and Charlie have orchestrated a little drama in which Bob plays the bad guy who sets out an extreme demand, and Charlie plays the good guy who, by contrast, appears reasonable. In many instances the extreme demand might have its intended effect of pressuring Liz and Pam into accepting Charlie's offer for fear that Bob might change Charlie's mind.

In this instance, however, Liz responds by saying, "That's interesting. . . ." She pauses for a second, giving herself a chance to think. Then she suddenly bursts out laughing and exclaims admiringly, "You guys are terrific! That is the *best* good guy—bad guy routine I've seen in years. Did you plan it, or was it just a coincidence? Seriously now, let's see if we can establish a *fair* price for the books."

Bob and Charlie don't quite know how to respond.

They can't really be offended, since Liz is complimenting them and they aren't sure whether she is serious. In any case, to pursue the tactic would be pointless. It works only when the other person is not aware of it. Having neutralized the tactic without alienating their opponents, Liz and Pam can proceed to discuss the purchase on its merits.

It is important that you bring up the tactic without appearing to attack the other side personally. Calling them liars or cheats does not make them more receptive to joint problem-solving negotiation. By showing admiration for Charlie and Bob's skill and making light of the tactic, Liz helps them save face. Her interest is not in scoring points, but in purchasing a set of law books for a fair price and in fostering a working relationship with an established law firm.

You should make it easy for the other side to drop their tactics. If they are being particularly rude, for instance, point it out by offering them an explanation or an excuse: "It sounds like you're having a rough day." If they threaten you, respond as one businesswoman did. Instead of challenging her opponent by saying "Don't threaten me," she asked in a calm and somewhat surprised tone, "You're not intending to threaten me, are you?" Her question of clarification offered her opponent a graceful way out. He took it, saying, "Who, me? No, I'm not threatening you." In case you have misinterpreted the other side's behavior, such an approach ensures that little if any harm will come of it.

Don't accuse the other side. Just make note of what they are doing. If a person constantly interrupts you, look him in the eye, use his name, and say "Mike, you interrupted me." Or ask "May I finish my sentence?" Use a nonconfrontational, matter-of-fact tone. If Mike does it again, patiently remind him, perhaps with a little gentle prodding, "Hey, you're interrupting me." Think of yourself as a friend giving him some useful feedback. Call him on his behavior—nicely.

Negotiate About the Negotiation

If bringing it up isn't sufficient, then you may need to have a full-fledged negotiation about the rules of the game.

Take your opponent aside and say, "It seems to me the way we're negotiating isn't going to lead to the kind of outcome we both want. We need to stop arguing about the issues and discuss the rules of the game." More informally, you could say, "Something's bothering me, and I'd like to talk it over with you."

Negotiate about the process just as you would about the substance. Identify *interests*, generate *options* for how best to negotiate, and discuss *standards* of fair behavior. If, for example, your opponent refuses to talk about anything except positions, you might explain, "My interest is in achieving a mutually satisfactory agreement efficiently and amicably. As I see it, in order for us to accomplish this we have to be willing to listen to each other, share information about our interests, and brainstorm together. We ought to be able to expand the pie, not just divide it up. If I understand your interests better, I can help you meet them, and you can do the same for me. Shall we give it a try?"

Without questioning your opponent's honesty, discuss the fairness of particular tactics: "What if *I* were to ask for additional concessions *after* we reached agreement? Would you consider that a legitimate tactic?"

Make a specific request for how you would like the

other side to change their behavior. If they continue to attack you personally, you can say calmly, "I'm willing to talk about this whenever you are willing to stop attacking me." If you are a CEO approached by a corporate raider seeking information about your company, you could say, "Look, if you're willing to rule out a hostile takeover, I'll be happy to talk candidly. Otherwise, I'll have to assume that you'll use the information I give you against me."

Once you have agreed on the rules, you can return to negotiating over the substance in a more constructive and productive manner.

The Turning Point

The turning point of the breakthrough method is when you change the game from positional bargaining to joint problem-solving. The key to changing the game is to reframe. Reframing means taking whatever your opponent says and directing it against the problem.

Consider how, in the example at the beginning of this chapter, the marketing chief might have used reframing to draw the budget director into a new game:

BUDGET DIRECTOR *(digging in to a position)*: I won't accept anything less than a ten percent cut in your budget. So let's get to it, okay?

MARKETING CHIEF *(asking a problem-solving question)*: I recognize the need to cut the company budget, and my department is prepared to contribute its share. Just help me understand why you need that much.

BUDGET DIRECTOR *(presenting a* fait accompli *and making a threat)*: The only way we can get the required savings is if each department takes a ten percent cut. I've already told the other department heads that you'll take the cut. If you don't, all the other deals will unravel and the president will hear about it.

MARKETING CHIEF *(ignoring the threat and reinterpreting the* fait accompli *as a problem to be solved)*: I understand what you're saying. If I were to cut any less, you'd have a big problem explaining that to all the other departments, right?

BUDGET DIRECTOR *(applying pressure)*: That's right. So let me put you down for that cut. Deal?

MARKETING CHIEF *(ignoring the pressure and reframing the problem as a joint opportunity)*: You know, we've got a real opportunity to save more than the ten percent. It would really help the company and make both of us look very good.

BUDGET DIRECTOR: Oh, what's that?

MARKETING CHIEF *(asking for advice)*: As you know, my department has just instituted a new plan that will bring about greater productivity and substantial cost savings. But there are start-up costs we've calculated at five percent of our budget. You have more experience in these matters than anyone else. How can we find the funds to implement the plan and still keep your other deals from unraveling?

BUDGET DIRECTOR: I don't know....

MARKETING CHIEF *(asking a problem-solving question)*: Could we explain to the other department heads that my department is taking a five percent cut this year in order to bring even greater savings next year?

BUDGET DIRECTOR: I don't think that will work.

MARKETING CHIEF *(asking a "what if" question)*: What if I were to commit to a specific figure of just how much we'll save next year?

BUDGET DIRECTOR: That might help. But that still doesn't solve the problem this year of where to make up the extra savings if you take only a partial cut. Look, I see what you're getting at, but what am I going to tell the president? It's not going to fly.

MARKETING CHIEF *(asking another "what if" question)*: What if I talked to the president and sold him on the idea?

BUDGET DIRECTOR: Good luck!

MARKETING CHIEF: I know. It may not be easy. But can I have your support?

BUDGET DIRECTOR: Let me see your plan again. I want to check and make sure your numbers aren't pie in the sky.

MARKETING CHIEF: I'll have it to you within the hour. Thanks for giving me this chance.

The marketing chief has not yet won the agreement she is seeking, but she has won the negotiation over the rules of the game. By reframing, she has turned a positional confrontation into a problem-solving negotiation. She and the budget director are now on their way toward negotiating a mutually satisfactory agreement.

4

Don't Push:

BUILD THEM A GOLDEN BRIDGE

Build your opponent a golden bridge to retreat across.

— *Sun Tzu*

You are now ready to reach agreement, having successfully suspended your reactions, defused the other side's emotions, and reframed their position. Still they may not agree. You face the barrier of their dissatisfaction. They may be asking themselves, "What's in it for me?" Things can still go wrong—as they all too often do.

A classic example is the failure of what might have been the world's biggest media merger. Every story has two sides; this is Al Neuharth's account of how he, in his own words, "blew the big one." In 1985, CBS was fighting a hostile takeover bid by media mogul Ted Turner. Neuharth, president of Gannett, had long had his eye on CBS

and had cultivated a cordial relationship with CBS president Tom Wyman. Neuharth arranged an exploratory
meeting with Wyman to discuss the possibility of a merger
that would enable CBS to resist the takeover.

After several meetings, the two men reached agreement on most of the basic issues. They decided that because
of his age and greater experience, Neuharth would become
chairman and CEO, while Wyman would become president and chief operating officer. In a draft press release
that Neuharth showed Wyman, Neuharth proposed that
the new company be called Universal Media.

Then executives from both companies began ironing
out the details. This is how Neuharth in his memoir describes the collapse of the talks:

A dozen bankers, lawyers and executives were assembled
around the long rectangular table. Tom and I sat side by side.
I was really pissed that people in this room for nearly three days
had been unable or unwilling to do what Wyman and I had
agreed upon. . . . I didn't waste a lot of time with social niceties:

"Tom and I thought it might help if the two CEOs got in on
the act and explained to all of you how to get this deal done.
It's pretty damn simple. . . . Tom and I have agreed on the management structure of the company. The directors will be seven
(CBS), seven (Gannett), and one (jointly selected). I will be chairman and CEO. Tom will be president and chief operating officer."

The CBS guys looked surprised and puzzled. Our people
nodded and smiled.

"You don't have to argue about this or even talk about it or
think about it. It's all settled."

Wyman looked uncomfortable. He sat up straight in his
chair. "Yes, we've agreed on that," he said a bit hesitantly. . . .

I sensed immediately that I had screwed up. I had come on
too directly and forcefully. Wyman's people were hearing this
news for the first time from me, not from him. . . . I should have
let Wyman explain the terms. He could have put a more gentle
face on it. I had satisfied my ego at the expense of crushing his.

Two days later Wyman telephoned to call off the deal. He objected to changing CBS's name and was angry because he had learned Neuharth had also been discussing a merger with Time Inc.

After Neuharth hung up the phone he turned to his executives and said, "The game's over. We lose. And he'll lose."

Obstacles to Agreement

After exploring each side's interests and the options for agreement, you may be ready to deal. But when you make your proposal, the other side may stall. Their resistance can take various forms: lack of interest in your proposals, vague statements, delays, reneging on agreements, or a flat no. In the case of the media merger, CBS's resistance manifested itself in the stymied negotiations between the two teams.

We often blame our negotiating counterpart's resistance on personality or basic nature, but behind the impasse usually lie some very good reasons. Consider the four most common ones:

Not their idea. The other side may reject your proposal simply because "it wasn't invented here." Neuharth failed to involve Wyman in choosing the new name and in presenting the merger terms to the assembled executives.

Unmet interests. You may be overlooking one of your counterpart's basic interests. CBS did not relish the thought of giving up its name.

Fear of losing face. No one wants to look bad to his or her constituents. Neuharth attributed the failure of the CBS-Gannett merger in large part to having made Wyman lose face in front of his own people.

Too much too fast. Your counterpart may resist because the prospect of agreeing appears overwhelming. The decision seems too big and the time too short. It may seem easier just to say no.

Your challenge is to persuade the other side to cross the chasm that lies between their position and the agreement you want. That chasm is filled with dissatisfaction, uncertainty, and fear.

Build a Golden Bridge

Frustrated by the other side's resistance, you may be tempted to push—to cajole, to insist, and to apply pressure. Neuharth pushed hard when the negotiations bogged down.

But pushing may actually make it more difficult for the other side to agree. It underscores the fact that the proposal is your idea, not theirs. It fails to address their unmet interests. It makes it harder for them to go along without appearing to be giving in to your pressure. And it makes the prospect of agreement seem, if anything, more overwhelming.

Consequently, the other side is likely to resist all the more. In fact, they may welcome your pressure, for it takes them off the hook of having to make a difficult decision. By pushing, Neuharth actually widened the chasm that Wyman had to cross in order to reach agreement.

Instead of pushing the other side toward an agreement, you need to do the opposite. You need to *draw* them in the direction you want them to move. Your job is to *build a golden bridge* across the chasm. You need to reframe a retreat from their position as an advance toward a better solution.

Take the simple example of how, as a teenager, filmmaker Steven Spielberg built a golden bridge for a tormenting bully:

> When I was about thirteen, one local bully gave me nothing but grief all year long. He would knock me down on the grass, or hold my head in the drinking fountain, or push my face in the dirt and give me bloody noses when we had to play football in phys. ed. . . . This was somebody I feared. He was my nemesis. . . . Then, I figured, if you can't beat him, try to get him to join you. So I said to him, "I'm trying to make a movie about fighting the Nazis, and I want you to play this war hero." At first, he laughed in my face, but later he said yes. He was this big fourteen-year-old who looked like John Wayne. I made him the squad leader in the film, with helmet, fatigues, and backpack. After that, he became my best friend.

Young Spielberg discovered the secret of building your adversary a golden bridge. He recognized that the bully needed to feel important. By offering the bully an alternative path to recognition, Spielberg successfully negotiated a ceasefire and turned him into a friend.

Building a golden bridge isn't easy. In a tough negotiation, you might ideally bring in a mediator to help resolve your differences. But that may be neither appropriate nor feasible. So, in the absence of a third party, you need to *mediate your own agreement.*

Instead of starting from where you are, which is everyone's natural instinct, you need to *start from where the other person is* in order to guide him toward an eventual agreement. One of the best descriptions of this process comes from a French novel. In it, a master diplomat explains, "I turn towards the other person; I become familiar with his situation; I mold myself on his destiny and, living in his place, I begin to experience his fortune and misfortune. Henceforth my concern is not so much to impose my point of view on him, as to persuade him to adopt the one I consider best for him—which always agrees with the interests of my own cause."

Building a golden bridge means making it easier for the other side to surmount the four common obstacles to agreement. It means actively involving them in devising a solution so that it becomes their idea, not just yours. It means satisfying their unmet interests. It means helping them save face; and it means making the process of negotiation as easy as possible.

Involve the Other Side

One of the most common negotiating mistakes is to announce that *you* have found the solution to the problem. City planners unveil their scheme for a new waste-disposal site without having involved the residents of the surrounding neighborhood; in response, a citizens' group immediately organizes to fight the project. Management announces a streamlined work plan without having consulted its employees; the workers secretly sabotage the plan. The national budget director and the President's chief of staff closet themselves with six congressional leaders and emerge with an agreed-upon set of budget cuts; members of Congress who weren't involved denounce the agreement and reject it in the subsequent vote. So, too, your negotiating counterparts are likely to reject your proposal if they have no role in shaping it.

Negotiation is not just a technical problem-solving exercise but a political process in which the different parties must participate and craft an agreement *together*. The process is just as important as the product. You may feel frustrated that negotiations take as long as they do, but remember that negotiation is a ritual—a ritual of participation. People see things differently when they become involved. They may make allowances they would not otherwise make. They may become comfortable with ideas they once rejected. As they infuse their ideas into the proposal, they make it their own.

Ask for and Build on Their Ideas

The great temptation in negotiation is to *tell*. Tell the other side the way to solve the problem. Tell them why your solution is good for them. Neuharth dealt with the sensitive issue of the new company name by telling Wyman in a draft press release that it should be called Universal Media. Not surprisingly, the idea didn't fly.

Negotiation is more about asking than it is about telling. The simplest way to involve the other side is to ask for their ideas. How would *they* solve the problem of reconciling both sides' interests? As Neuharth later acknowledged, he should have asked Wyman for his ideas before telling him what the new name should be. Not only would

Neuharth have gotten Wyman involved, but he would have discovered how much importance CBS attached to keeping its name.

Once you have elicited your counterpart's ideas, you need to build on them. This doesn't mean accepting them as they are. Rather, select the ideas you find most constructive, and starting with them, head off in the direction you want to go. It is easier to get your boss to change her position if you say "Building on your idea, what if we . . . ?" Or "I got this idea from something you said at the meeting the other day. . . ." Or "As a follow-up to our discussion this morning, it occurred to me that . . ." Show the other side how your proposal stems from or relates to one of *their* ideas.

Building on their ideas does not mean shortchanging your own. It means building a bridge from their thinking back to yours. Keep in mind the seventeenth-century abbot about whom the Pope said, "When the conversation began, he was always of my opinion, and when it ended, I was always of his."

Ask for Constructive Criticism

As you develop your ideas, keep the other side involved by inviting their criticism. Stress that you are asking not for a yes or no decision but for feedback. Encourage constructive comments by asking problem-solving questions, such as "Which interests of yours does this approach fail to satisfy?" "In what respect is it not fair?" "How would you improve on it?" and "Is there any way we can make it better for your side without making it worse for mine?"

Once you have elicited their suggestions, consider creating a joint draft that incorporates their ideas as well as your own. Then run it by them for further comments. In a multiparty negotiation, show it to all the relevant participants and invite their suggestions. Then revise the draft, and if necessary, ask for more criticism. Gradually you will build consensus. The process is a little like creating a mural together—the other side paints a few strokes, you do, their boss does, yours does. Everybody who gets involved begins to think of the draft as their own.

Offer Them a Choice

If the other side resists telling you their ideas or giving you feedback on yours, try to involve them by offering them a choice. For instance, if they have been putting off talking with you, begin by asking for small decisions: "Is ten o'clock on Tuesday better for you than three o'clock on Wednesday?" and "Would you prefer to meet at your office or mine?"

If they refuse to explore options for breaking the impasse, offer them a list of alternatives to choose from. If you are deadlocked over price, for example, say, "We can resolve the difference between your asking price and my offer by having an appraiser decide, *or* I can pay the difference with assets other than cash, *or* I can spread out the payments over time. Which approach would you prefer?" It may be easier for the other side to choose between A, B, and C than to invent D.

Once they select an alternative, it becomes their idea. Take the example of the homeowner who was negotiating an agreement with a general contractor. Worried that the remodeling work on her house might take much longer than she planned, the homeowner proposed a twenty percent penalty for failure to finish on time. But the contractor refused. So she challenged him: "Okay, *you* name a date you're absolutely certain the job will be done." Put on the spot, the contractor picked a date three months after the scheduled completion. The homeowner then asked, "Okay, now will you agree to the clause?" Because she was only asking him to live up to his own worst-case estimate, the contractor agreed.

The process of working together with an opponent can be long and arduous, but the rewards can be great. Remember the Chinese proverb: "Tell me, I may listen. Teach me, I may remember. Involve me, I will do it."

Satisfy Unmet Interests

Even if the other side is fully involved in the process of shaping an agreement, they still may resist coming to terms. Often their resistance stems from an unmet interest that you have overlooked.

Take the acquisitions negotiator for Campbell Soup Company who was trying to buy an extremely successful restaurant from its owner-manager. Campbell's was interested in starting a chain of such restaurants. The acquisitions negotiator started by making what he thought was a fair offer, but the owner rejected it. Over the ensuing six weeks the negotiator increased the offer several times but to no avail. The owner would not even make a counteroffer. The talks were at an impasse, and the negotiator was on the verge of giving up. He blamed the deadlock on the owner's difficult personality.

But then the negotiator decided to probe a little. In his next meeting with the owner, he backed off from his single-minded pursuit of a deal and encouraged the owner to discuss his reservations about selling the business. The owner said, "This business is my baby. And it has made me famous. I'm not sure I want to sell it and become part of your company. For one thing, I like running my own show. You're going to have to pay me a lot to make it worth my while to give it all up." The negotiator came to appreciate the owner's strong needs for autonomy and recognition, interests that were clearly not met by a deal in which the owner became a company employee.

So the negotiator asked the owner: "What if you don't become our employee? This would be a little unusual, but what if we form a joint venture together to own and operate the restaurant? Campbell's would purchase, say, eighty percent of the stock from you, and you would keep twenty percent. You would be president of the joint venture; you'd stay in charge. And we would agree to buy your twenty percent at some future time. The longer you stay, the more we would pay for your stock. Would something like this meet your needs?"

The owner's response was positive, and a deal was soon struck. His needs for recognition and autonomy were fulfilled, as was his interest in a decent price. Campbell's was able to acquire the restaurant at a reasonable cost and to retain the owner long enough to benefit from his successful management formula.

This story illustrates how useful it is to look for a creative solution. More important, it shows how easy it is to miss such a solution by overlooking the other side's unmet interests. To address these interests as the Campbell's negotiator did, you have to jettison three common assumptions: that the other side is irrational and can't be satisfied;

that all they basically want is money; and that you can't meet their needs without undermining yours.

Don't Dismiss Them as Irrational

When you are frustrated by an inflexible opponent, it is easy to blame the impasse on his or her irrational nature: "My boss is crazy. No one can deal with him," or "Teenagers are just hopeless. It's no use reasoning with them." If you conclude that your opponent is impossible to deal with, you will not bother to probe for unmet interests.

It is easiest to reach this conclusion with hostagetakers: "You can't negotiate with terrorists—they're madmen." Certainly, their behavior may be irrational from our perspective, but it may make perfect sense from *theirs*. As long as there is a logical connection *in their eyes* between their interests and their actions, then we can influence them. One leading hostage negotiator, who represents corporations worldwide whenever their executives are seized, says, "They're all rational. Everyone negotiates. Even the 'dregs' give value for money." If hostage-takers are susceptible to being influenced, then your boss and teenager probably are too.

So don't give up easily. Put yourself in the other side's shoes and ask yourself honestly: "Would I agree to this if I were them? Why not?" And remember that their values may differ from yours, which might lead them to reject what you consider acceptable. If you take a hard look, as the Campbell's negotiator did, you may well uncover interests that make it understandable from their perspective to say no.

Try to address the other side's objections and satisfy their interests while still meeting your own. Terrorists, for example, are usually motivated by the deep desire to get public recognition for their cause. Often the secret to persuading them to release hostages is to let them know that their message has been heard, and that killing the hostages would only discredit them in the eyes of the public. Many seemingly intractable hostage-taking incidents have ended after the terrorists received air time on TV and radio.

Don't Overlook Basic Human Needs

We often assume, as the Campbell's negotiator did at first, that the other side is interested only in money or something equally tangible. We miss the *intangible* motivations that drive their behavior—their basic human needs. Everyone has a need for security and a deep desire for recognition. Everyone wants to identify with some group and have control over their own fate. Nations and ethnic groups have basic needs too. If unmet, these needs can block agreement.

By satisfying the other person's basic human needs, you can often turn the person around. The Campbell's negotiator was able to fulfill the restaurant owner's needs for recognition and autonomy. The young Steven Spielberg found a way to meet the bully's need to feel important. A hostage-taking in Boston ended after the authorities guaranteed that the hostage-taker would not be physically harmed. An impasse over a Wisconsin bank purchase was broken when the buyer agreed to keep the seller's name on the bank. An ethnic conflict in Italy's Trentino-Alto Adige region was defused when the German-speaking minority was granted cultural and administrative autonomy.

Don't Assume a Fixed Pie

Even if you have identified the other person's unmet interests, you may believe you cannot satisfy them without frustrating your own. You may be falsely assuming a "fixed pie"—that more for that person means less for you. Frequently, however, you can expand the pie and satisfy the person's unmet interests at no cost and possibly some benefit to yourself.

Look for low-cost, high-benefit trades. The most common way to expand the pie is to make a low-cost, high-benefit trade. Identify items you could give the other side that are of high benefit to them but low cost to you. In return, seek items that are of high benefit to you but low cost to them.

Consider a negotiation between an American businessman and a Moscow cabdriver. In broken Russian, the businessman inquired what the fare would be from the airport to the Rossia hotel. "Forty rubles," replied the cabbie. The price—equivalent at the time to sixty dollars—seemed high to the businessman, but when he asked another taxi driver, he was quoted the same fare. He then went back into the airport and bought a twenty-dollar bottle of vodka at a foreign currency store. He offered it to the first cabbie in lieu of payment and the cabbie eagerly accepted. Why? Because the Russian would have had to wait in a four-hour line to buy the same bottle in a local liquor store. The vodka was low-cost to the American, high-benefit to the Russian. The cab ride was low-cost to the Russian and high-benefit to the American.

Use an if-then formula. Another way to expand the pie is to use an "if-then" formula. Suppose that you are a marketing consultant negotiating with a client over your fee. You would normally charge fifteen thousand dollars, but your client is unwilling to pay more than ten thousand. Her resistance stems largely from uncertainty about whether your efforts will truly help her. Instead of trying to persuade her that she is wrong, address her skepticism with an if-then formula: "What do you say we make my fee ten thousand dollars as a base, but *if* your sales increase twenty percent over the next six months, *then* you agree to add a ten-thousand-dollar bonus?" Your client readily agrees, because the increased sales would make it easy to justify paying you the bonus. You take a risk, but if you are successful, you stand to earn even more than you originally requested. In sum, don't fight the other side's skepticism; take advantage of it by inventing a pie-expanding solution.

Help Them Save Face

Even if you are able to satisfy the other side's substantive interests, they still may not agree. After all, a negotiation does not take place in a social vacuum. There is always a constituency or audience whose opinion the other side cares about—their boss, their organization, their colleagues, their family and friends, or their own internal critic. Naturally they don't want them to think they have given in. If they have previously taken a public position and then do an about-face, their constituents might say, "You sold out!" "What kind of negotiator are you?" or "You let him rob us blind!" The other side's inflexibility may stem from constraints imposed by their constituents, rather than from their own concerns.

You may think, "Let them worry about *their* critics, and I'll worry about mine." But since their people can obstruct the agreement you want, it is your job to help the other side deal with them. Criticism from constituents typically boils down to two arguments: that your counterpart has backed down and that the proposed agreement is unsatisfactory. Your challenge is to help your counterpart avoid both criticisms.

Help Them Back Away Without Backing Down

Face-saving is at the core of the negotiation process. There is a popular misconception that a face-saving gesture is just a cosmetic effort made at the end of a negotiation to boost the other person's ego. But face is much more than ego. It is shorthand for people's self-worth, their dignity, their sense of honor, their wish to act consistently with their principles and past statements—plus, of course, their desire to look good to others. All these may be threatened if they have to change their position. Your success in persuading them to do so will depend on how well you help them save face.

Consider the face-saving skill shown by French statesman Georges Clemenceau in negotiating for a statuette in an Oriental bazaar. The shopkeeper offered it to Clemenceau for "only" seventy-five rupees "because it's you." The Frenchman responded with a counteroffer of forty-five rupees. The haggling continued, but Clemenceau stuck to his initial offer. Eventually, the shopkeeper threw up his hands and protested, "Impossible! I'd rather give it to you!" "Done!" replied Clemenceau, pocketing the statuette. "You are exceptionally kind, and I thank you, but such a gift could only come from a friend. I hope you will not be insulted if I offer you a gift in return." The perplexed shopkeeper said he would not. "Here," said Clemenceau, seeking to help him save face, "are forty-five rupees for you to use in charitable works." The shopkeeper accepted the money, and they parted on excellent terms.

Show how circumstances have changed. One face-saving approach is to explain that originally your counterpart may have been right but that circumstances have changed. Suppose your most important customer insists on revisions in your company's standard sales contract but the lawyer at company headquarters has told you there will be no alterations. Instead of challenging the lawyer's decision directly, identify new conditions that enable the lawyer to justify a new approach: "Your no-changes policy has always been the right one for a regulated marketplace. Now that the Feds have deregulated this sector, however, we're facing much tougher competition. Do we really want to risk losing one of our biggest customers?"

Ask for a third-party recommendation. A time-honored method of face-saving is to call in a third party—a mediator, an independent expert, a mutual boss or friend. A proposal that is unacceptable coming from you may be acceptable if it comes from a third party.

Take the avid fisherman who wanted to buy a cabin in the North Woods. The owner insisted on an unrealistically high figure—$45,000—and announced he would not bargain. The fisherman tried hard to change the owner's mind but to no avail. So the fisherman finally said, "Okay, I'll pay whatever an appraiser determines to be the fair price for the house." The owner responded, "All right, but *I* pick the appraiser." The fisherman countered, "Okay, you pick an appraiser, and I'll pick an appraiser, and together the two can select a third." The owner agreed. They each identified appraisers who in turn chose the president of the local appraisers' society. Under the watchful eyes of his peers, he came up with a figure of $38,000. Muttering that the appraiser didn't know what he was doing, the stubborn owner nevertheless agreed to sell the cabin at that price. Having kept his pledge not to bargain, he hadn't lost any face.

Point to a standard of fairness. In the absence of a third party, you can use the next-best thing: a fair standard. Suppose you are at loggerheads with an insurance claims agent over compensation for your stolen car. She refuses to pay more than $5,000 but you think $7,000 is fair. So you say, "Why don't we let the marketplace decide? You check the classified ads for similar cars, and I'll do the same. Let's talk again tomorrow." With the new information on hand, you agree on a figure of $6,500. She doesn't feel she is backing down, since she is simply deferring to the market price. She also has a legitimate explanation if her supervisor should question why she agreed to pay you the additional $1,500.

Help Write Their Victory Speech

Your counterpart's constituents may attack the proposed agreement as unsatisfactory. So think about how your counterpart can present it to them in the most positive light, perhaps even as a victory. What could you offer that would help make your counterpart's explanation a victory speech?

President John F. Kennedy and his advisers asked themselves this question in October 1962, as they searched for a way to make it easier for Soviet Premier Nikita Khrushchev to withdraw Soviet missiles from Cuba. Kennedy decided to offer Khrushchev his personal pledge that the United States would not invade Cuba. Since Kennedy had no intention of invading anyway, the promise was easy to make. But it allowed Khrushchev to announce to his constituents in the Communist world that he had successfully safeguarded the Cuban revolution from American attack. He was able to justify his decision to withdraw the missiles on the grounds that they had served their purpose.

Anticipate what your counterpart's critics are likely to say and present persuasive counterarguments. If, for example, you are an investment banker negotiating with your boss for a raise and bonus, think what your boss's partners might say if he agreed to your proposal: "You're being too lavish with the firm's money." "You're going to make us look bad when our people find out how well yours did." Then think of answers your boss could give: "He deserves it. He brought in five million dollars' worth of business last year." "If we don't reward him for his hard work, we'll lose him to the competition." When you ask your boss for more money, prepare him by raising likely criticisms and presenting the counterarguments.

At little or no cost to yourself, you may be able to help the other side reframe a retreat as an advance. Suppose, for example, you are dealing with a union leader who has pledged to bring back a ten percent wage increase. You might agree to give him a four percent increase this year and a three percent increase for the next two years. He can tell his membership that he succeeded in obtaining a ten percent increase—over three years. Or suppose you are buying a house from a couple who are determined to get

$200,000 because that's what they paid for it, even though it is now worth only $180,000. You might agree to pay $200,000 but stretch out the payments over time so that the deal is equivalent to a $180,000 immediate payment.

Don't forget the value of giving credit. Even if the solution is your idea, consider letting the other side share the credit—or take all of it. In Washington, D.C., a city full of politicians eager to claim good ideas as their own, there is a saying that goes: "There's no limit to how much you can accomplish in this town if you are willing to allow someone else to take the credit." The same holds true in negotiations. Take the bride who wanted to register for china. Her fiancé resisted, saying, "We don't need all that crockery." The china became a sore subject. In a goodwill gesture he accompanied her to the store, where he saw a pattern he liked. She happily agreed to his selection and gave him credit for the choice. He proudly announced to their families and friends that *he* had selected the china.

Even if there is nothing you can give the other side, you can often shape appearances so that they do not seem to lose. When British Prime Minister Benjamin Disraeli was pestered by a supporter who wanted a noble title, Disraeli told him: "You know I cannot give you a baronetcy, but you can tell your friends that I offered you one and you refused it. That's much better."

Go Slow to Go Fast

Even if you can satisfy the other side's interests and help them save face, they still may not agree because the process of reaching agreement seems too difficult. Too much needs to be decided in too short a time.

Your job is to make the process easy. Go slow in order to go fast. Think of yourself as a guide helping a client afraid of heights climb a steep mountain. Break the journey into small stages, pace your client, stop to rest when necessary, and look back periodically at how far you have come.

Guide Them Step-by-Step

If reaching agreement on the whole package seems impossible at first, try breaking the agreement up into steps. A step-by-step approach has the merit of making the impossible gradually seem possible. Each partial agreement can open up opportunities that were not evident at the outset.

Consider how far a step-by-step approach took American diplomat Charles Thayer in negotiating with a German prison director at the outbreak of World War II. Thayer, whose mission was to deliver some belongings and supplies to a British vice-consul being held prisoner, recalled:

He [the prison director] had the British vice-consul brought from his cell, and one by one I handed over the items: pyjamas, shirts, socks, and a toilet kit.... I then produced a bottle of sherry, explaining that the vice-consul should have it served before his luncheon. The director said nothing, but took the bottle submissively. Next I produced a bottle of champagne which, I said, should be properly iced with the vice-consul's dinner. The director shifted uneasily but remained silent. Next came a bottle of gin, another of vermouth, and a cocktail shaker.

This, I explained, was for the vice-consul's evening martini. "Now, you take one part of vermouth," I began, turning to the director, "and four parts of gin, add plenty of ice—" But I had reached the end of my tiny steps.

"*Verdammt!*" the director exploded. "I am willing to serve sherry and champagne and even gin to this prisoner, but he can damn well mix his own martinis."

If Thayer had presented all his requests at once, the prison director would undoubtedly have rejected the whole lot. By taking a step-by-step approach, Thayer substantially accomplished his mission.

To break the ice at the start of a tense negotiation, begin, as Thayer did, with the issue that is easiest for you to agree on. By moving progressively from the easier to the more difficult issues, you can get the other side into the habit of saying yes and show them that agreement is possible.

If the other side is particularly skeptical, consider starting with an experiment. Suppose you have devised a solid proposal for a new project but your boss is reluctant to give you the go-ahead. To your boss, it seems simpler and safer to stick with the tried and true. To make it easier, make the agreement experimental: "Can we carry out a pilot project with one department?" or "Can we try it out for one month?" By reducing the risk, an experimental agreement makes it easier for your counterpart to say yes.

When you are in the thick of the negotiation, it is easy to lose perspective and grow disheartened. Identifying the expanding areas of agreement and the shrinking areas of disagreement can generate a sense of momentum. Pause at each step to sum up progress: "So we've essentially agreed on the product and price. All we have to decide is how we share the costs of service and delivery."

Don't Ask for a Final Commitment Until the End

Sometimes the step-by-step approach won't work because the other side is reluctant to make even a small agreement, thinking, "If I give an inch, you'll take a mile." If this is the case, don't press them for an immediate concession. Set them at ease by reassuring them that they need not make a final commitment until the very end when they can see exactly what they will get in return.

This is what President Jimmy Carter did during the 1978 Camp David negotiations on the Middle East. Both Israeli Prime Minister Menachem Begin and Egyptian President Anwar Sadat were reluctant to budge from their stated positions, fearing that any concession would be perceived as a sign of weakness. So Carter did not ask them to change their positions until the end of the thirteen days of peace talks. During that time he focused their attention on criticizing and continually improving an American discussion draft. After twenty-three drafts there seemed to be no way to make the draft better for one side without making it worse for the other. Only then did Carter ask Begin and Sadat for a decision. Instead of having to make many painful decisions along the way, each leader had to make only one at the end. Instead of facing a slippery slope, each could see exactly what he was going to get in return for his concessions. Begin saw that in exchange for relinquishing the Sinai, he would get peace with Egypt. Sadat saw that in return for making peace with Israel, he would get the Sinai back. Both leaders said yes.

If the other side resists a step-by-step approach, make clear that *nothing* is agreed until *everything* is agreed.

Don't Rush to the Finish

The closing phase of a negotiation is often characterized by a rush. The business meeting is coming to an end. A strike deadline is pending. One of the parties needs to catch a plane. Or you may simply sense an agreement is near and begin to sprint toward it like a runner at the end of a race.

Whatever the reason for the rush, it is easy to make mistakes in this atmosphere. If you hurry the other side, they will often react by exploding over something trivial or by suddenly finding fault with part of the agreement. In order not to lose them, you need to slow down, back off, and give them a chance to think.

Encourage them to consult with their constituents. Their constituents may have instructed them to maintain a rigid position. If they come back with a very different agreement, their people may well reject it. A caucus allows the other side to educate their constituents about the merits of the proposed agreement and to secure their support.

In the rush, it is also easy to conclude that you have reached agreement when in fact you haven't. As your lawyers set to drafting the contract the following morning, they may discover that you and your counterpart have different interpretations of the agreement. This can lead to accusations of bad faith that leave you worse off than if you hadn't declared agreement in the first place.

There is a simple way to avoid this problem. When you think you have reached agreement, take a moment to sum up: "Let's make sure we both have the same understanding of what we have agreed on." Then go over each issue carefully. If possible, set down your agreement in writing. Movie mogul Samuel Goldwyn once quipped, "A verbal contract isn't worth the paper it's written on." Whatever you do, make sure the terms are as clear and specific as possible. A little bit of clarity at this stage can prevent a lot of unnecessary misunderstanding later.

Across the Bridge

Building a golden bridge involves much more than making the other side an attractive proposal. First, it means involving them in crafting the agreement. Second, it means looking beyond their obvious interests, such as money, to address their more intangible needs, such as recognition or autonomy. Third, it means helping them save face as they back away from their initial position; it means finding a way for them to present the agreement to their constituents as a victory. And last, it means going slow to go fast, guiding them step-by-step across the bridge.

You have now made it as easy as possible for the other side to say yes. If they cross the bridge, congratulations. If they don't, however, you need to make it as *hard* as possible for them to say no. That is the subject of the next chapter.

5

Don't Escalate:

USE POWER TO EDUCATE

The best general is the one who never fights.

—*Sun Tzu*

What if, despite all your efforts to build the other side a golden bridge, they still refuse to come to agreement? You have one more barrier to break through: their power plays. Even if your proposed agreement is attractive, they may still think of the negotiation as a game where one side wins and the other loses. They may judge how much they win by how much you lose. They may be confident that they can dominate you into submission.

You may conclude that you have no choice but to play their power game. In the power game, you switch from listening and acknowledging to threatening, from reframing the other side's position to insisting on your own, and from building a golden bridge to forcing them down the gangplank. You use all your power to force them to do what you want them to do. You try to get your difficult co-worker fired, you sue your delinquent customer, you go on strike against an intransigent management, or you go to war against your national adversary.

You escalate not only your means but also your ends. As you invest more of your resources in the battle, you naturally want more from your opponent to compensate for your efforts. Your goal shifts from mutual satisfaction to victory.

The power game is supposed to work as follows: You threaten or try to coerce the other side and then they back down. However, unless you have a decisive power advantage, they usually resist and fight back. They get angry and hostile, reversing your attempts to disarm them. They cling even more stubbornly to their position, frustrating your efforts to change the game. They become increasingly resistant to reaching agreement, not only because you may be asking for more but because agreement would now mean accepting defeat.

The harder you make it for them to say no, the harder you make it for them to say yes. That is the power paradox.

You are thus forced at great cost to try to impose a solution on the other side. As they strike back, you typically escalate into a costly struggle. In pursuing the lawsuit, strike, or war, you spend a great deal of time and money, not to mention blood, sweat, and tears.

You can easily end up with a lose-lose outcome instead of the win-win result you sought. The company that sues may lose a valued customer, the union that goes on strike may force the company into bankruptcy, and the nation that goes to war may bog down in a ruinous stalemate. "An eye for an eye and we all go blind," Mahatma Gandhi once said.

Even if you win the battle, you may lose the war. In the process you may destroy your relationship with the other side. And they will often find a way to renege or retaliate the next time they are in a position of power. Warfare—in its military, corporate, or domestic forms— is a high-priced method of handling disputes. That is why more than two thousand years ago, the great Chinese strategist Sun Tzu wrote: "To win one hundred victories in one hundred battles is not the acme of skill. To subdue the enemy without fighting is the acme of skill."

How can you use power to bring your opponent to terms without ending up in a costly fight? How can you use power constructively rather than destructively? How can you overcome the power paradox?

Use Power to Educate

The key mistake we make when we feel frustrated is to abandon the problem-solving game and turn to the power game instead.

Overcoming the power paradox means making it easier for the other side to say yes *at the same time* that you make it harder for them to say no. Making it easy to say yes requires problem-solving negotiation; making it hard to say no requires exercising power. You don't need to choose between the two. You can do both.

Treat the exercise of power as an integral part of the problem-solving negotiation. Use power to bring the other side to the table. Instead of seeking victory, aim for mutual satisfaction. *Use power to bring them to their senses, not to their knees.*

If the other side refuses to come to terms despite all your efforts, it is usually because they believe they can win. They believe that their best alternative to negotiation— their BATNA—is superior to your golden bridge. You need to convince them that they are wrong.

Use your power to *educate* the other side that the only way for them to win is for *both* of you to win together. Assume the mind-set of a respectful counselor. Act as if they have simply miscalculated how best to achieve their interests. Focus their attention on their interest in avoiding the negative consequences of no agreement. Don't try to impose your terms on them. Seek instead to shape their choice so that they make a decision that is in their interest *and* yours.

Using power to educate the other side works in tandem with building them a golden bridge. The first underscores the costs of no agreement, while the second highlights the benefits of agreement. The other side faces a choice between accepting the consequences of no agreement and crossing the bridge. Your job is to keep sharpening that choice until they recognize that the best way to satisfy their interests is to cross the bridge.

Let Them Know the Consequences

If the other side does not understand the consequences of failing to reach agreement, you should begin by making it clear how serious these are.

Ask Reality-Testing Questions

The best and cheapest way to educate the other side is to let them teach themselves. Ask questions designed to get them to think through the impact of not reaching agreement. *Let reality be their teacher.*

When Chrysler Corporation was on the verge of bankruptcy in 1979, company president Lee Iacocca tried to negotiate with Congress for a loan guarantee. But most lawmakers strongly believed that government should not be in the business of bailing out private enterprises. In subsequent congressional hearings, Iacocca tried to bring skeptical legislators to their senses. To focus attention on the consequences of rejecting Chrysler's appeal, he asked "reality-testing" questions: "Would this country really be better off if Chrysler folded and the nation's unemployment rate went up another half of one percent overnight? Would free enterprise really be served if Chrysler failed and tens of thousands of jobs were lost abroad?"

Citing the Treasury Department's estimate of how much the layoffs would cost the government in unemployment insurance and welfare payments in the first year alone, Iacocca told the lawmakers: "You guys have a choice. Do you want to pay the 2.7 billion dollars now, or do you want to guarantee half that amount with a good chance of getting it all back?"

In essence, Iacocca was asking "Do you want to accept the consequences of no agreement, or would you prefer to cross the golden bridge?" While the legislators opposed helping Chrysler on ideological grounds, they changed their minds when they recognized the real choice facing them. As Iacocca later wrote, when the member of Congress "realized how many people in his constituency de-pended upon Chrysler for their living, it was farewell ideology." Iacocca got the 1.5-billion-dollar loan guarantee he needed.

The three most common reality-testing questions are:

"What do you think will happen if we don't agree?" The most obvious question is the one Iacocca asked Congress: "What will the costs be if we can't reach agreement?" If your negotiating counterpart seems to be missing part of the picture, bring it up in the form of a question: "Have you considered the possibility that a prolonged strike will put this company into bankruptcy and we will all lose our jobs?" or "Are you aware how serious the consequences will be for both of us if we don't settle this issue?" If the other side has not focused on this problem previously or has underestimated the consequences, they may now begin to appreciate just how attractive your golden bridge really is.

"What do you think I will do?" If you think your counterpart might be underestimating the strength of your BATNA, ask, "If we can't reach agreement, what do you expect me to do to satisfy my interests?" or "What would you advise me to do?" A boss faced with an employee who has been missing work might ask, "What do you expect me to do if you're absent again?" or "What would *you* do if your employee was absent and you couldn't get the project done?" If you want to put it less personally, refer to your constituency. A union leader can ask a management counterpart: "How do you think the employees will feel about losing their health benefits, and what do you think they'll do about it?"

If the other side has threatened you, ask them how they think you will respond if they carry out the threat: "Sure,

you could go on strike, but if you do that, what would
you expect us to do? Do you think we'll just sit on our
hands?" Use questions to show them that you are not as
vulnerable to threats as they may think and that your logical countermove would leave both sides worse off. "We
have a six-month inventory, and we'll be able to keep the
plant running with management personnel. It will hurt us
for sure, but it will hurt the workers more. So where will
that leave us?" Let them know that if you reported their
threat to your constituency, it would only backfire: "If I
convey that to my board members, they'll feel they're being
blackmailed and you won't find them easier to deal with."

"What will you do?" If you think the other side is overestimating their alternative, question them about it: "What
are you likely to do in the absence of agreement? How
much will that cost you? How will that satisfy your interests?" Obviously they will tend to exaggerate the strength
of their BATNA, so probe a little to expose its negative
points: "You could take this matter to court, of course, but
how long will that take? And what about the legal ex-
penses? And even if you're sure you're right, will a jury
necessarily see it your way?"

Warn, Don't Threaten

Asking questions may not always be enough to educate
your counterpart about the realities of failing to reach
agreement. The next step is to use a direct statement of
what will happen. Before proceeding with your BATNA,
you should let the other side know what you intend to do.
You want to give them a chance to reconsider their refusal
to negotiate. Indeed, a warning can be more effective than
actually using your BATNA—since your alternative may

loom larger in your opponent's imagination than it will in reality.

You need to be careful, however, not to threaten the other side. A threat can easily backfire, changing the issue from a matter of dollars and cents to a test of their power and reputation. The raised stakes will make them fight back much harder. A direct threat will also tend to unify their organization against you. Internal differences will disappear as everyone joins forces to fight you, their common enemy.

How can you let the other side know about your BATNA in a way that propels them to the negotiating table, not the battleground? The key lies in framing what you say as a *warning* rather than a threat. At first sight, a warning appears to be similar to a threat, since both convey the negative consequences of no agreement. But there is a critical, if subtle, distinction: A threat appears subjective and confrontational, while a warning appears objective and respectful.

A threat is an announcement of your intention to inflict pain, injury, or punishment on the other side. It is a negative promise. A warning, in contrast, is an advance notice of danger. A threat comes across as what *you will do* to them if they do not agree. A warning comes across as *what will happen* if agreement is not reached. A warning, in other words, puts some distance between you and your BATNA. It objectifies the consequences of no agreement so that they appear to result from the situation itself. It is easier for your opponent to bend to objective reality than to back down to you personally.

While a threat is confrontational in manner, a warning is delivered with respect. Present your information in a neutral tone and let the other side decide. The more dire the warning, the more respect you need to show.

A threat is telling a recalcitrant production director:

"If you don't agree to increase production, I'm going to take it up with headquarters." The production director is likely to react: "Who do you think you are, telling me how to run my department?" The director may get angry, and you may be dragged into a corporate brawl. A warning, in contrast, is telling the director: "If the agreed-upon production quota isn't met, this division will really suffer, and we'll all be in trouble with headquarters." This way you are more likely to induce the director to return to try to solve the problem with you.

Sometimes you need to use a deadline to force a decision. Yet an arbitrary deadline may be interpreted as a threat. It is more effective to build in "natural" deadlines, which serve as objective warnings. Such deadlines might be this year's budget decision, the quarterly board of directors meeting, an upcoming press report, or the approach of Christmas holidays. These dates appear to be beyond your control, and thus are easier for your counterpart to accept.

Demonstrate Your BATNA

If the other side ignores your warning, you will need to take the next step: Make your power credible by demonstrating your BATNA. A demonstration shows what you plan to do without your having to carry it out. It educates the other side at minimum cost to you and minimum pain to them.

In Japan, for instance, workers often carry on a "strike" while they continue working. They wear black armbands in order to let management know the depth of their grievances. The armbands also remind management how much potential power the employees wield over the economic future of the company. Such symbolic strikes have proven surprisingly effective in bringing management to the table for serious negotiations about workers' grievances.

If your BATNA is to go to court, you can demonstrate it by involving a lawyer in the negotiation. One neighborhood association, intent on persuading a resistant highway department to build underpasses rather than highly visible overpasses, hired a prominent lawyer to accompany its spokesperson as he delivered a petition to the department. Not a word was said about taking the dispute to court, but the message came through loud and clear. The highway department decided to reverse its original decision.

To demonstrate your BATNA in the midst of negotiations, you can walk out. This tactic is not to be used lightly. You should not be bluffing but rather sending the other side and their constituents a strong signal that you are serious about resorting to your BATNA. When you walk out, you do not need to slam the door. Just say, "I'm sorry, but the way in which we have been negotiating is not likely to lead to a constructive outcome. I'm ready to negotiate anytime you are. Here's my phone number. Please give me a call when you're ready. Until then, I guess I'll have to pursue my alternatives." Leave the door open for the other side to call you back, or for your boss to call their boss, or for a third party to bring you back together.

Another way to demonstrate your BATNA is to prepare to carry it out so that the other side discovers your plans in advance. Take the situation of an exclusive department store that had a discriminatory employment policy, hiring minorities only for the most menial jobs. A community organization protested, but the store refused to negotiate. In response, the organization mobilized three thousand minority shoppers and planned to bus them, dressed up in their finest clothes, to the store on one of its busiest Saturdays. The shoppers would browse for hours, keeping the salespeople occupied. The store's regular clientele would enter the store, take one look at the milling crowd, and leave. The leaders of the community organization included in their planning sessions someone who they knew would leak their plans to the store. When the store managers learned of the scheme, they requested immediate negotiations with the community organization and quickly agreed to hire a sizable number of minority salespeople and executive trainees.

Remember that power, like beauty, exists in the eyes of the beholder. If your BATNA is to have its intended educational effect of bringing the other side back to the table, they need to be impressed with its reality.

Use Your BATNA, Defuse Their Reaction

If your opponent still refuses to negotiate, you have no choice but to use your BATNA. The dissatisfied workers would strike. The neighborhood association would file a lawsuit against the highway department. The community organization would carry out its shopping expedition to the department store. The marketing chief would ask headquarters to order the manufacturing division to increase production.

The problem, however, is that your open exercise of power is likely to provoke the other side into fighting back, even when their doing so makes no sense. Their emotions may take over, blinding them to the costs of fighting and the benefits of negotiating. Their "irrational" resistance may end up frustrating your attempt to educate them through the use of power.

How you use power is therefore all-important. *The more power you use, the more you need to defuse the other side's resistance.*

Deploy Your BATNA Without Provoking

Power lends itself to abuse. The exercise of power can easily become an escape valve for your pent-up feelings of frustration and anger. You probably have a natural human desire to make the other side pay for all the grief they have caused you. Yet for every action you take, there is likely to be an equal and opposite reaction on their part. "The more brutal your methods," wrote Sir Basil Liddell Hart, a noted British military strategist, "the more bitter you will make your opponents, with the natural result of hardening the resistance you are trying to overcome."

Use the minimum power necessary. Next to not using your BATNA at all, the best approach is to use it as little as possible. Use the minimum power necessary to persuade your opponent to return to the negotiating table. Usually this means exhausting all your alternatives before escalating. At the outset of the Cuban missile crisis, President Kennedy decided against ordering an immediate air strike on the Soviet missiles in Cuba. He wanted to avoid provoking Premier Khrushchev into ordering a counterstrike against U.S. forces in Berlin or Turkey that might, in turn, escalate into World War III. To display his power without ratcheting up the stakes, Kennedy resorted first to a naval blockade around Cuba. His strategy paid off. The crisis was resolved through negotiation, not war.

The more restraint you exercise, the less negative the other side's reaction is likely to be. If you are a striking union, keep the strike peaceful; stop your hotheads from engaging in physical violence or industrial sabotage. If you are the employer, think hard before hiring replacements for the strikers. Go out of your way not to provoke the other side, remembering that your ultimate goal is to bring them to the negotiating table.

When faced with a Communist rebellion in Malaysia in 1948, Winston Churchill summoned Field Marshal Templar and gave him full authority to do whatever he needed to quash the rebellion. Churchill had one piece of advice, however, for the field marshal: "Absolute power, Templar . . . Heady stuff . . . Use it sparingly."

Use legitimate means. The more legitimate your use of power, the less likely the other side will resist it, and the more likely it will induce them to negotiate. In the case of the discriminatory department store, for example, shopping was perfectly legal, and management could not keep out the minority shoppers without generating negative publicity about the store and its hiring policies. In the Cuban missile crisis, President Kennedy chose to use a naval blockade, in good part because he believed it would be a more legitimate means than an air strike. Legitimacy depersonalizes the use of power; your opponent is less likely to feel personally challenged and compelled to react.

Neutralize Their Attacks

A power contest is a two-way street. The other side may strike at you in retaliation for your power move or simply in order to force you to accept their terms. You will need to defend yourself. Counterattacking, however, will often result in a futile confrontation. The more effective approach is to *neutralize* your opponent's attack without striking back.

If you think your customer will threaten to go over your head to get a better deal, talk to your boss beforehand. Secure her commitment that she will refer the customer back to you. When the customer makes his threat, you are ready: "Please feel free to talk to my boss. I have already discussed the matter with her, and I'm confident she will tell you the same thing I have." Without attacking the customer, *neutralize* his ability to coerce you.

Consider the case of a coal mine with troubled labor-management relations. The mine was beset by bomb threats telephoned in to the switchboard just as the shifts were changing. Management would have to respond by closing the mine while a search was conducted. Finally, mine officials hit on the idea of instructing the switchboard operator to record the calls and tell callers: "Your voice is being recorded. How can I help you?" The first recorded bomb threat was played to the assembled miners, who were asked to let management know if they recognized the voice. After that, the number of bomb threats dropped off drastically. Management had effectively neutralized the caller's tactic.

Or consider an international example. In 1948, Soviet leader Joseph Stalin blockaded West Berlin, demanding that Allied troops leave the city. The Western powers considered breaking the blockade with an armed convoy but feared triggering World War III. Instead, they chose to neutralize the blockade by mounting an enormous airlift of food and supplies to the beleaguered Berliners. Realizing the blockade was not working, Stalin finally called it off and agreed to negotiate.

As each of these situations illustrates, your challenge is

to foil the other side's attack without attacking back. Your goal is not to punish them but to show them that they can satisfy their interests only through negotiation.

Tap the Third Force

You may not have enough leverage by yourself. Fortunately, almost every negotiation takes place within a larger community that constitutes a potential "third force" in your negotiation. Involving other people is often the most effective way to deter your opponent's attacks and bring about agreement without provoking a counterreaction.

Build a coalition. Whether you are inducing a dictator, a department store, or a difficult boss to negotiate, it is helpful to build a powerful coalition of supporters. The United States stood together in the Berlin crisis with Great Britain and France. The neighborhood association obtained the services of a prominent lawyer. The minority community organization was able to mobilize three thousand shoppers. In identifying potential allies, consider those most likely to sympathize with and lend support to your cause: a trusted friend or relative, a longstanding client, an organization that shares your goals, or someone who has experienced similar problems with your opponent.

While we naturally think of turning to our friends and allies, we rarely consider appealing to the other side's constituency—their family, friends, co-workers, and clients. The other side may not listen to you, but their constituents might. And the other side may well listen to those constituents if they urge negotiations. In domestic hostage negotiations, for example, the police often use family members and friends to talk the hostage-taker into acting sensibly; in international cases, nations with ties to the hostage-taking group are often asked to intercede.

In addition to your allies and theirs, you can mobilize the people in the middle, the undecideds, the neutrals. If you are negotiating with your departmental rival over who will take the lead on a new project, the person in the middle may be your mutual boss. If you are a community organization trying to negotiate with a recalcitrant developer, you may turn to the media for coverage and supportive editorials.

Use third parties to stop attacks. The presence of a third party can deter your opponent from threatening or attacking you. When children are quarreling, the watchful eye of a parent will often prevent fisticuffs. When the general public is watching, even a dictatorial government may hesitate before using violence on protesters.

Consider an extraordinary negotiation. In 1943, hundreds of German women married to Jewish men marched for more than a week in the streets of Berlin. They sought to free their husbands from Nazi prisons where the men were awaiting transport to the gas chambers. The Nazis trained machine guns on the women, but they would not budge. They presented the Nazis with a dilemma: Release the prisoners or use violence on "Aryan" women in full view of a citizenry whose support and morale the Nazis were anxious to preserve. In the end, the most barbaric of governments chose the first option, and approximately fifteen hundred Jews were saved from death. The women were able to deploy their BATNA—the street march—while inhibiting a negative reaction—a machine-gun slaughter—because of the presence of third parties—the German public.

Use third parties to promote negotiation. Third parties can
also induce your opponent to negotiate with you. The CEO
can tell you and your rival vice-president that you must
resolve your dispute within a week. A judge can call you
and your opposing counsel into chambers and press you
to reach a settlement out of court. Sometimes just the
knowledge that others are watching is enough to bring
your opponent to the table.

A third party can also help you settle your dispute by
mediating. A mediator can help each of you to understand
the other's interests and can suggest possible options for
agreement. Your opponent will usually find it easier to
accept a mediator's solution than to give in to you. And if
you are not on speaking terms, a third party can bring you
together. The mediator may be a mutual friend, your common boss, a community leader, or a professional neutral.

If the other side refuses to agree to your proposal, you
can elicit the support of others in making them see its
wisdom. Consider the intervention approach commonly
used in persuading alcoholics to seek treatment. A long-
suffering wife, for instance, was faced with an alcoholic
husband who repeatedly broke his promises to stop drink-
ing. In desperation she turned to others for help: his
children, siblings, closest friends, and employer. Together
they confronted the alcoholic to persuade him to seek treatment. One by one they told him how much he meant to
them and recounted specific incidents of dangerous driving, personal violence, or embarrassing behavior. They
then collectively insisted he seek help. To make his decision
easier, they had already prepared a list of treatment centers
and made reservations for him at each. Faced with this
outpouring of concern and support, he at last decided to
accept the help he needed. The wife's effort would not have

been enough; it took the urging of his friends, relatives, and colleagues. As the old adage puts it: "If one person tells you that you have a tail, you laugh. If three people tell you, you turn around to look!"

Other parties are more likely to help if you can show them you have a legitimate case. Bring to bear independent standards, such as past precedent, equity, company rules, and the law. Just being right is usually not enough, so frame your dispute as one in which the issue or principle is important to the third party. If you turn to your boss, you are more likely to win support if you can show how your boss's personal interests or the larger interests of the company are at stake.

If the other party is not inclined to help bring your opponent to agreement, you may need to give them a reason to care. Consider the tactic adopted by tenants living in a slum building. They were trying to persuade the landlord to repair the broken plumbing, but he refused to listen. So the tenants decided to picket. Rather than carry their signs around the building or the landlord's office, they went to his home in an exclusive suburb. Within minutes the landlord was deluged with calls from his neighbors, who said, "I don't care how you make your money. Just get those people off our sidewalk." Not surprisingly, he agreed to repair the plumbing.

When resorting to your BATNA, don't overlook the useful role third parties can play in bringing the other side back to the table. If you exert your power through them, you are less likely to trigger a strong negative reaction from your opponent.

Keep Sharpening Their Choice

As you educate the other side about the costs of no agreement, you need to remind them continually of the golden bridge you have built for them. When they refuse to negotiate, you understandably feel tempted to draw up the bridge—to rescind your last best offer. In fact, you ought to leave your most generous offer on the table in full view. Nothing will do more to reduce resistance than the possibility of an attractive way out.

Your power to bring the other side to terms comes not from the costs you are able to impose but from the *contrast* between the consequences of no agreement and the allure of the golden bridge. Your job is to keep sharpening the contrast until they realize that the best way to satisfy their interests is to cross the bridge.

Let Them Know They Have a Way Out

Power is useless if it drives the other side into a corner and makes them resist you with all their might. Leaving your opponent a way out is a time-honored precept. In the military chronicles of ancient China, the story is recorded of a general who surrounded a group of rebels at a city called Yuan Wu. Unable to capture the city, the general was reprimanded by his king: "Now you have massed troops and encircled the enemy, who is determined to fight to the death. This is no strategy! You should lift the siege. Let them know that an escape route is open, and they will flee and disperse. Then any village constable will be able to capture them!" The general followed this advice and took Yuan Wu.

Although you may assume the other side knows of the way out, they may have become convinced that the way out no longer exists. A bank robber who has taken hostages may believe that, because he has shot a police officer in a gunfight, he has nothing more to lose from killing his hostages. It is the job of the police negotiator to reassure him that he can still salvage something by negotiating. A teenager who has stolen money from his parents to buy drugs may not believe he will ever be welcomed back into the family; it is the parents' challenge to convince him that he can come home.

It is easy for the other side to misread your attempt to educate them through power as an attempt to defeat them. You need to reassure them constantly that your aim is mutual satisfaction, not victory. In a negotiation over a raise, your boss could interpret your bringing up an attractive job offer as a threat to leave. You will need to go out of your way to reassure your boss that you want to stay. *For every ounce of power you use, you need to add an ounce of conciliation.*

Let Them Choose

Paradoxically, just when the other side appears to be coming around, you are well advised to back off and let them make their own decision. Respect their freedom to choose between the consequences of no agreement and the golden bridge. In the final analysis, the choice must be theirs. When family members and friends confront an alcoholic in an organized intervention, they urge him to seek help, describe the consequences of his not agreeing, but ultimately respect his freedom to choose.

Don't just give the other side an either/or decision. Allow them to shape the details. Although the family may have packed the alcoholic's bags and made reservations for his treatment, they leave him with a choice of at least two treatment centers. This lets him assume ownership of the decision.

Even When You Can Win, Negotiate

An imposed outcome is an unstable one. Even if you have a decisive power advantage, you should think twice before lunging for victory and imposing a humiliating settlement on the other side. Not only will they resist all the more, but they may try to undermine or reverse the outcome at the first opportunity. Earlier this century, the world learned this lesson at enormous cost; an imposed peace after World War I broke down and led to World War II.

The most stable and satisfactory outcomes, even for the stronger party, are usually those achieved by negotiation. Benjamin Disraeli, the nineteenth-century British prime minister, summed up the lesson for negotiators: "Next to knowing when to seize an advantage, the next most important thing is knowing when to forgo an advantage." In the midst of a power contest, it is vital for you to remember that your purpose is not victory through superior power but satisfaction through superior negotiation.

Consider how a small city in Texas sought to negotiate with a major oil company over the taxes to be paid by an oil refinery just outside the city limits. The citizens felt dissatisfied because their schools were poor, the roads bad, and community services inadequate. The city councilors pleaded with the company for a larger contribution to the city coffers, but the company refused—even though its tax rate was much lower than the rate paid by individual citizens.

There seemed little the city councilors could do. The company appeared to have all the power in the negotiation. It was one of the world's largest corporations, it was the town's biggest employer, and it was represented by shrewd and tough lawyers.

In desperation, the citizens held a meeting to decide what to do. After much discussion, a local lawyer came up with an unusual proposal: "State law allows the town to expand the city limits if three quarters of the residents approve. Why don't we just annex the land on which the oil refinery stands? Applying the city tax rate should bring in the extra revenue we need." The idea was adopted, and the town held a referendum that was overwhelmingly approved.

The city now had a powerful BATNA. The councilors decided, however, *not* to put it into effect. They didn't want to antagonize the company—they just wanted it to assume a fairer share of the city's tax burden. So when they sat down to negotiate with the company's lawyers, they said, "We recognize all you have done for the good of the town. We couldn't survive without you. But, as you know, people feel very unhappy about our schools and roads, and they don't see why your company shouldn't pay at the same rate as everyone else. The law allows us to annex the refinery land, in which case you would have to pay the city tax rate. But we'd rather reach an agreement that satisfies your interests better."

The councilors went on to discuss mutually beneficial ways to make the tax less burdensome. They offered a tax break on future investment in the refinery, recognizing that this would boost the city's economy. Knowing of the company's campaign to attract its suppliers to relocate near the refinery, they offered a five-year tax holiday for new industries. In short, they tried to build a golden bridge for the company.

What could the company do? The referendum made it impossible to ignore the town's needs. The company's BATNA—moving the refinery—was far too costly. The company could, of course, retaliate by scaling down operations and canceling its contributions to local charities. But the councilors weren't just trying to squeeze it for money; the city was facing a genuine financial crisis. The councilors defused the company's reaction by going out of their way not to impose a solution and by seeking instead to satisfy the company's interests.

In the end, the city and the company came to terms. The company agreed to increase its tax contribution from $300,000 to $2,300,000 a year. Rather than continuing to deteriorate, relations between the city and the company began to improve.

Forge a Lasting Agreement

Assuming you are successful in bringing the other side to terms, you are now faced with one final challenge: translating their newfound willingness to negotiate into a firm and lasting agreement.

Keep Implementation in Mind

Reaching agreement is one thing; implementing the agreement is another. The other side may fail to carry out the terms. A delinquent customer may promise you, "The check will be in the mail tomorrow." A bankrupt businessperson may claim, "I'm sure receipts will come in next week." But can you rely on their words?

You need to design an agreement that induces the other side to keep their word and protects you if they don't. You don't need to act distrustful; act *independently* of trust.

Design the deal to minimize your risks. Don't just rely on a court to enforce your agreement; litigation can be long and costly. If you have doubts about the other side's reliability, structure the deal so you don't have to carry out your side of the agreement until they fulfill theirs. If you are a buyer, arrange to delay your payments or put them in escrow until the seller has delivered all the promised goods. If you have recently made a sale to an erratic customer, don't build up a lot of inventory for their sake. Wait until they develop a track record of prompt payment.

To protect yourself further, you can build guarantees into the agreement. Instead of relying on someone's promise to buy your house or company, ask for a nonrefundable security deposit. If you are being hired into an uncertain job, propose a "golden parachute" clause that specifies what you will receive if the company folds or you are fired.

Make it more difficult for your counterpart to back out by involving others. Try to secure the signatures of the key players on the other side. Invite people or institutions that your counterpart cares about to witness the agreement. Announce the deal publicly.

Don't let the other person treat your doubts as a personal attack. If the person says "Trust me," you can answer "Of course I trust you," and explain that it is just normal business practice: "Personally I am sure nothing will go wrong with our arrangements, but my lawyer insists on the routine of including the following guarantees." Or, if your future employer insists a handshake and an oral promise of a golden parachute is sufficient, say, "You're absolutely right, and I have full faith in what you are saying. Writing a memo to the file will be helpful, however, if you're promoted tomorrow and I get a new boss."

Build in a dispute resolution procedure. Guarantees offer you a *final* resort if your counterpart breaks the agreement—but they don't give you a *first* resort. For that, you need to establish in advance a dispute resolution procedure. Your contract should spell out exactly what will happen if one party feels the other is not living up to the terms of the agreement.

A typical dispute resolution procedure might specify that you will first try to negotiate a resolution of your differences. If, after thirty days, you are unable to reach agreement, you will call in a mediator. If the mediator is unsuccessful in thirty more days, you will submit your dispute to binding arbitration by a mutually acceptable third party. Oil companies about to engage in a joint venture have set up partnership committees to handle any disagreements that arise; if a dispute persists, it is referred to two senior executives, one from each company, who try to mediate a settlement. Only if that fails do the companies resort to arbitration. You should consider including a dispute resolution procedure in every agreement you make.

Reaffirm the Relationship

A difficult negotiation can easily strain your relationship. If the other side leaves the table with sour feelings, they may not do a good job of selling the deal to their constituents or implementing it. They may carry out the letter but not the spirit of the agreement.

It is in your interest for your counterpart to feel as

satisfied as possible at the conclusion of the negotiation. Although you may feel elated at your success, don't crow. In the wake of the Cuban missile crisis, President Kennedy issued strict instructions to his Cabinet officers not to claim victory. He did not want to make it harder for Premier Khrushchev to justify to his comrades his decision to withdraw the missiles.

Be generous at the very end. Resist the natural temptation to fight over the last crumb. As a professional hostage negotiator put it: "We save some flexibility for the end because we like them to win the last round. We're easier at the end than they expect because we want them to think they did well." Your counterpart's satisfaction can pay off handsomely in the agreement's implementation, as well as in future negotiations.

After a difficult negotiation, you may feel that you never want to see the other side again. Yet as long as you are dependent on them to carry out the terms of the accord, it is wise to preserve a good working relationship. Gracious words and symbolic gestures can help. If appropriate, organize a signing ceremony and a celebration for both sides. Check in with the other side regularly to make sure they think you are keeping up your side of the bargain. And deal promptly with any grievances they raise. The best guarantee of a lasting agreement is a good working relationship.

Aim for Mutual Satisfaction, Not Victory

The eminent Prussian military strategist Karl von Clausewitz looked upon war as a continuation of politics by other means. Similarly, you should treat power as a continuation of problem-solving negotiation by other means. Everything flows from that. You aim for mutual satisfaction instead of victory. You use power to educate rather than fight. You let your counterpart know about the consequences of no agreement—through reality-testing questions, warnings rather than threats, and, if necessary, demonstrations of your power.

If you do have to use your BATNA, you use the minimum power necessary to induce the other side to return to the table. You deploy your BATNA without provoking and neutralize their attacks without attacking back. You work to defuse their reaction so they do not turn your use of power into a costly and futile battle.

You remind the other side continually that the golden bridge is open to them. You do not seek to impose a solution but rather to help them make the choice that is best for them—and for you. In short, you use power to educate, not escalate.

PART III

Turning Adversaries
into Partners

Conclusion

TURNING ADVERSARIES INTO PARTNERS

There is a story of a man who left seventeen camels to his three sons. He left half the camels to his eldest son, a third to his middle son, and a ninth to his youngest. The three set to dividing up their inheritance but soon despaired of their ability to negotiate a solution—because seventeen could not be divided by two or three or nine. The sons approached a wise old woman. After pondering the problem, the old woman said, "See what happens if you take *my* camel." So then the sons had eighteen camels. The eldest son took his half—that was nine. The middle son took his third—that was six. And the youngest son took his ninth—that was two. Nine and six and two made seventeen. They had one camel left over. They gave it back to the wise old woman.

Like the seventeen camels, your negotiations will often seem intractable. Like the wise old woman, you will need to step back from the negotiation, look at the problem from a fresh angle, and find an eighteenth camel.

The breakthrough strategy can be your eighteenth camel. It allows you to step to the balcony and view your difficult negotiation from a new perspective. You break through by going around the other side's resistance, approaching them indirectly, acting contrary to their expectations. The theme throughout is to treat your opponent with respect—not as an object to be pushed, but as a person to be persuaded. Rather than trying to change the other side's thinking by direct pressure, you change the environment in which they make decisions. You let them draw their own conclusions and choose for themselves. *Your goal is not to win over them, but to win them over.*

To accomplish this goal, you need to resist normal human temptations and do the opposite of what you naturally feel like doing. You need to suspend your reaction when you feel like striking back, to listen when you feel like talking back, to ask questions when you feel like telling your opponent the answers, to bridge your differences when you feel like pushing for your way, and to educate when you feel like escalating.

Breakthrough negotiation is hard work. Successful negotiators are patient and persistent. Progress usually comes gradually. Small breakthroughs can add up to a major breakthrough. In the end, even negotiations that once seemed impossible can often yield a mutually satisfactory agreement.

To illustrate how all five steps of the strategy hang together, consider two quite different examples: a negotiation with an employer over a raise and a negotiation with an armed criminal over hostages.

A Salary Negotiation

Think about how a difficult negotiation over salary might proceed:

EMPLOYEE: Mr. Pierce, can I talk to you for a minute?
EMPLOYER: If it's about that raise, Elizabeth, don't waste my time. The answer is no.
EMPLOYEE: I haven't even asked you yet.
EMPLOYER: You don't have to ask. There's no money in the budget.
EMPLOYEE: But it's been a year and a half since my last raise.
EMPLOYER: Didn't you hear what I said? There's no money in the budget. Have I made myself perfectly clear?

Consider the ways this conversation might go. Action and reaction could lead either to the employee giving in or to a destructive argument that ends with the employee quitting. Alternatively, the employee could suspend her reaction by counting to ten. On the balcony, she remembers her dual interests in getting the raise and maintaining a working relationship with her difficult boss. Instead of arguing with him, she does the opposite and steps to his side of the issue:

EMPLOYEE: I realize we've got a very tight budget and that we're all under a lot of pressure now. I'm not asking you to take money out of the budget to give me a raise.
EMPLOYER: You're not?
EMPLOYEE: No, I don't want to put you on the spot. I know you're doing the best you can for all of us under trying circumstances.
EMPLOYER: That's right. I wish I had the money but I just don't. ... So what is it you're asking for?

EMPLOYEE: I'd just like a few minutes of your time at your convenience to discuss how I'm doing for you, what I could do better, and what I can expect in return knowing there's no money in the budget right now.

EMPLOYER: Well, I suppose it wouldn't hurt to talk. Come around tomorrow at ten but, remember, a raise is out of the question.

The employee has not yet won agreement on a raise, but she has defused some of her boss's resistance. She has created a more positive climate in which they can then negotiate. Their next meeting proceeds as follows:

EMPLOYEE: I appreciate your taking the time to meet. I've been thinking about what you were saying about the tight budget we're operating under. I was wondering if there was any way I could help us save money by taking on additional responsibilities. . . .

EMPLOYER: Well, that's an interesting question. Let's see now . . .

Instead of rejecting her boss's position on the raise, the employee reframes it into a discussion of how to meet his underlying interest of cutting costs. Only after this conversation does the employee bring up again the possibility of a raise:

EMPLOYEE: Now I realize a raise right now is out of the question, but *if* I'm able to help us cut costs, could we then think about compensating me out of those savings for the extra tasks I'll be undertaking—understanding, of course, that we'll stay within budget?

EMPLOYER: I'm not sure any of this will actually work.

EMPLOYEE: What if we made it a bonus conditional on realized savings?

And they are on their way toward an agreement that will satisfy both their needs. The employee is busy building her boss a golden bridge. If the employer *still* resists, the employee may need to let him know about her BATNA, in this case, the other job offer she has sought and obtained. If she wants to stay and maintain a good working relationship with her boss, she needs to avoid provoking him:

EMPLOYEE: Mr. Pierce, I'd like your advice. I've enjoyed working here and I'd very much like to continue, but I'm having a lot of trouble paying for my kids' college tuition on my current salary. I've received a job offer that would provide the extra funds. Ideally I'd like to stay on here. Is there any way we can work this out?

Such an approach might wake the employer up to the reality of losing a valuable employee and make the golden bridge seem very attractive. If negotiating with this employer seems too easy, consider how the breakthrough strategy was applied in one of the most difficult situations imaginable: a hostage negotiation with an armed criminal.

A Hostage Negotiation

On Thursday morning, October 14, 1982, scores of police converged on the nation's second-largest medical facility, Kings County Hospital in Brooklyn, New York. A convicted armed robber named Larry Van Dyke was holed up in a basement locker room with five hospital employees. Van Dyke, who had just had a cast removed from a broken arm, had seized a gun from a corrections officer, shot and wounded him, and tried to escape. Cornered by police,

Van Dyke had taken hostages. Almost immediately he had let one person go, instructing him to tell police: "I want out of here or I'm going to start killing people."

A decade earlier the police would probably have handled such an incident by using force. "In the old, old days," a police captain recalled, "we'd surround the place, give the guy the bullhorn, fire the tear gas, put on some type of flak jacket, and engage the guy in a firefight."

But instead of fighting, the police decided to talk. Detective Lieutenant Robert J. Louden, a trained hostage negotiator, began a conversation with Van Dyke by shouting through the closed locker-room door: "How ya doin'? My name's Bob and I'm here to see what's going on. I'm here to help sort this out and help us get out of this mess. What's your name?"

Van Dyke replied, "My name's Larry Van Dyke and I've got a whole roomful of people. I've got nothing to lose. I'm not going back to jail. You've got thirty minutes to give me my freedom."

Louden did not reject the demand or the deadline, but reframed them instead as aspirations: "I'll see what I can do. I'll look into it for you and get back to you as soon as I can. As you know, these things take time. It's not a decision I can make. In the meantime, is there anything *I* can get for you?" Louden was trying to refocus Van Dyke's attention on what was achievable.

As Louden was talking, a backup negotiator stood behind him. The backup's job was to prompt Louden with questions, pass him messages, and make sure he kept his emotional balance. It was Louden's way of going to the balcony.

Van Dyke warned that if the police tried an assault, he would kill the hostages. Louden assured him that no one was going to hurt him. "You don't know how we operate," the detective said. "In ten years no one's ever been hurt. We don't storm doors. It's not like TV." Van Dyke's lawyer counseled his client: "Larry, no one is going to hurt you. In three hundred cases, the hostage negotiation unit has never hurt anyone."

Van Dyke threatened to break out of the room with his hostages. Louden told him: "Larry, you're better off staying in. You've got us locked out and we've got you locked in. We've got plenty of people out here. We don't want to use force, but we will if we need to. You're smart. You know how the game is played. Let's see if we can work this out."

Louden asked open-ended questions to find out what Van Dyke was thinking and what he wanted: "How did you get into this mess? How can we sort it out?" Van Dyke started complaining about corruption and abuse in the state prison system. Louden listened sympathetically, saying, "I understand how you feel," "I've heard similar things from others," and "Because you've raised it, we may be able to launch an investigation into the corruption." He was trying to build rapport with Van Dyke, acknowledging his points and agreeing where possible; in effect, Louden stepped to Van Dyke's side.

Van Dyke demanded to talk to Bella English, a reporter from the *Daily News* whose writing he admired. Louden agreed to help find her and persuaded Van Dyke to accept a field telephone to make communication easier.

Step by step, the detective made progress. Bella English was flown to the site in a police helicopter. "We want you to go on the phone," Louden told her, "but please don't use negative words like 'hostage' or 'jail.' "

English introduced herself to Van Dyke and asked him why he wanted to talk to her. "Because you're a fair reporter," he replied. He told her that he faced a prison

sentence of twenty-five years to life on robbery charges.
Coached by Louden, English tried to reassure Van Dyke
that this was not necessarily so. Shortly thereafter, Van
Dyke agreed to let one hostage go as soon as he received
pillows, blankets, and coffee. At 4:15 P.M., the hostage
emerged.

Four hours later, Van Dyke agreed to let another hostage go if radio station WOR allowed English to broadcast
his gripes about prison conditions. A few minutes after the
broadcast, Van Dyke released the second hostage. "That
was real good," Van Dyke told English. "You just saved a
life." "No," English replied, "*you* just saved a life."

Van Dyke then agreed to free a third hostage if WABC-
TV broadcast a live message during the eleven o'clock evening news. The station complied at the Police Department's
request. On the air, the freed hostage conveyed a message
of love from Van Dyke to his wife and said no one would
be hurt, as long as the police didn't provoke anything.

Shortly after midnight, however, Van Dyke's mood
changed. The police heard him threatening a hostage:
"Old man, get on your knees. I got a gun to his head here.
I don't want to hurt anybody but if they treat me ridiculous,
I'll act ridiculous." Van Dyke tried to fix the blame on
Louden: "This ain't going quick enough. I'm going to kill
these people and it will be your fault."

But Louden deflected the blame: "Bullshit, Larry.
We're here to help. We're all in this together. But if you
do that, it's not us. It's you. Now let's see if we can work
this out." Louden constantly sought to redirect attention
back to the problem.

On Friday morning, tensions rose. Van Dyke had asked
for the morning newspapers, but became angry when he
saw reports that he had been accused of informing on
fellow inmates. "They blew it!" he screamed in rage. "They

said I snitched on inmates and guards. Guards, correct. Inmates, no." He said he had been forced by prison guards to entrap other guards in drug deals, and claimed he would be killed if he was returned to state custody.

Louden tried to calm Van Dyke, addressing his basic need for security: "I know you're not an informant. Whoever gave that statement was wrong. All the media can hear me saying that. Let me see if I can work it so you don't have to go back to a *state* pen."

Louden contacted federal and state corrections officials to explore whether Van Dyke could be transferred to a federal penitentiary. The tension began to dissipate when Mike Borum, a deputy state corrections commissioner, came to tell Van Dyke that he would try to arrange a transfer. Van Dyke told his cousin, a corrections officer who had been brought to the scene: "I'm thinking of surrendering. They offered me a good deal." Louden had built Van Dyke a golden bridge to retreat across.

Van Dyke agreed to release a fourth hostage if WABC-TV and WINS radio agreed to broadcast the release live, and also let Van Dyke tell his side of the story. On the air he complained about state prison conditions: "I have been beat up. I have been set up."

Four hours later Van Dyke became morose, insisting he didn't want to return to jail. He told Louden: "I've got nothing to lose. We're going to play Russian roulette." Louden tried to reassure him and talked soothingly to him through the night.

Early Saturday morning, Van Dyke finally agreed to release the final hostage in return for press coverage and Borum's public promise of a transfer. At eight o'clock Louden was able to report to Van Dyke that Borum was making his statement on WABC-TV. Twenty-five minutes later, the last hostage was released. At eight-thirty, Van

Dyke came out to surrender. He was granted his request to talk with the press. "I'm not a madman," he said. "I'm a man that was trying to get freedom. . . . I got caught. I'm here." Then police took him away to the Metropolitan Correction Center, a federal detention center in lower Manhattan.

After forty-seven hours, one of the longest and most dramatic hostage incidents in New York City history was over. "Personally, I couldn't have held out much longer," said Louden, hoarse and weary.

The outcome was a victory for the police, who were able to win the release of hostages, prevent bloodshed, and take the criminal back into custody. Louden said that he and other members of his team had finally persuaded Van Dyke to give up by "trying to build trust and confidence, trying to establish that we could treat each other as human beings and help each other out of this okay."

Van Dyke didn't win his freedom, but he won a public promise to be transferred to a federal prison. After he surrendered, Van Dyke gave police the highest compliment they could have hoped for: "They shot straight with me," he said.

Just as the best general never has to fight, so the police never had to use force. They used their power not to attack Van Dyke, but to contain him and educate him that his best alternative lay in surrendering peacefully. They brought him to his senses, not his knees.

The Five Steps of Breakthrough Negotiation

Whether you are negotiating with your boss, a hostage-taker, or your teenager, the basic principles remain the same. In summary, the five steps of breakthrough negotiation are.

1. Go to the Balcony. The first step is not to control the other person's behavior. It is to control your own. When the other person says no or launches an attack, you may be stunned into giving in or counterattacking. So suspend your reaction by naming the game. Then buy yourself time to think. Use the time to reflect about your interests and your BATNA. Throughout the negotiation, keep your eyes on the prize. Instead of getting mad or getting even, focus on getting what you want. Don't react: Go to the balcony.

2. Step to Their Side. Before you can negotiate, you need to create a favorable climate. You need to defuse the anger, fear, hostility, and suspicion on the other side. They expect you to attack or to resist. So do the opposite. Listen to them, acknowledge their points, and agree with them wherever you can. Acknowledge their authority and competence too. Don't argue: Step to their side.

3. Reframe. The next challenge is to change the game. When the other side takes a hard-line position, you may be tempted to reject it, but this usually only leads them to dig in further. Instead direct their attention to the challenge of meeting each side's interests. Take whatever they say and reframe it as an attempt to deal with the problem. Ask problem-solving questions, such as "Why is it that you want that?" or "What would you do if you were in my shoes?" or "What if we were to . . . ?" Rather than trying to teach the other side yourself, let the problem be their teacher. Reframe their tactics, too, by going around their stone walls, deflecting their attacks, and exposing their tricks. Don't reject: Reframe.

4. Build Them a Golden Bridge. At last you're ready to negotiate. The other side, however, may stall, not yet convinced of the benefits of agreement. You may be tempted to push and insist, but this will probably lead them to harden and resist. Instead, do the opposite—draw them in the direction you would like them to go. Think of yourself as a mediator whose job is to make it easy for them to say yes. Involve them in the process, incorporating their ideas. Try to identify and satisfy their unmet interests, particularly their basic human needs. Help them save face and make the outcome appear as a victory for them. Go slow to go fast. Don't push: Build them a golden bridge.

5. Use Power to Educate. If the other side still resists and thinks they can win without negotiating, you need to educate them to the contrary. You need to make it hard for them to say no. You could use threats and force, but these often backfire; if you push them into a corner, they will likely lash out, throwing even more resources into the fight against you. Instead, educate them about the costs of not agreeing. Ask reality-testing questions, warn rather than threaten, and demonstrate your BATNA. Use it only if necessary, and minimize their resistance by exercising restraint and reassuring them that your goal is mutual satisfaction, not victory. Make sure they know the golden bridge is always open. Don't escalate: Use power to educate.

From Adversaries to Partners

It takes two to tangle, but it takes only one to begin to untangle a knotty situation. It is within your power to transform even your most difficult relationships. Your greatest power is the power to change the game—from face-to-face confrontation to side-by-side joint problem-solving. Obstructing the path are formidable barriers: your natural reactions, their hostile emotions, their positional behavior, their strong dissatisfaction, and their perceived power. You can overcome these barriers by applying the strategy of breakthrough negotiation. You don't have to take no for an answer.

During the American Civil War, Abraham Lincoln made a speech in which he referred sympathetically to the Southern rebels. An elderly lady, a staunch Unionist, upbraided him for speaking kindly of his enemies when he ought to be thinking of destroying them. His reply was classic: "Why, madam," Lincoln answered, "do I not destroy my enemies when I make them my friends?"

The breakthrough strategy is designed to do precisely that—to destroy your adversaries by turning them into your negotiating partners.

PREPARATION WORKSHEET

INTERESTS Mine	Theirs
1.	1.
2.	2.
3.	3.

OPTIONS
1.   4.
2.   5.
3.   6.

STANDARDS
1.   4.
2.   5.
3.   6.

BATNA Mine	Theirs

PROPOSALS Aspire To	Content With	Live With

ANALYTICAL TABLE OF CONTENTS

I. GETTING READY

Overview: Breaking Through Barriers to Cooperation

Joint Problem-Solving
Five Barriers to Cooperation
   Your reaction
   Their emotion
   Their position
   Their dissatisfaction
   Their power
The Breakthrough Strategy

Prologue: Prepare, Prepare, Prepare

Mapping Out the Way to Agreement
  1. Interests
    Figure out your interests
    Figure out their interests
  2. Options
  3. Standards
  4. Alternatives
    Identify your BATNA

4. Don't Push: BUILD THEM A GOLDEN BRIDGE

END NOTES

Prologue

The ideas in this section—interests, options, standards, and alternatives—derive from *Getting to Yes* by Roger Fisher and William Ury (Boston: Houghton Mifflin, 1981). For a more extensive treatment, see Chapters 3, 4, 5, and 6.

Your BATNA is your walkaway alternative: The term BATNA comes from Roger Fisher and William Ury, *op. cit.*

1. Go to the Balcony

"The balcony" is a metaphor: I owe the phrase "go to the balcony" to my friend Professor Ronald Heifetz, who uses it in his courses on leadership at Harvard's John F. Kennedy School of Government.

You need to look for multiple clues: For a good discussion of recognizing lies, see Paul Ekman, *Telling Lies* (New York: Norton, 1985) and Suzette Haden Elgin, *Success with the Gentle Art of Verbal Self-Defense* (Englewood Cliffs, New Jersey: Prentice Hall, 1989), pp. 28–29.

One of the most celebrated political images: Sergei Khrushchev, personal communication with author, February 1989.

"I was carrying him home": Quoted in "When Bad Bosses Happen to Good People," Jane Ciabattari, *Working Woman*, July 1989, pp. 88–89.

A movie producer: This example is adapted from a story told by screenwriter and humorist Larry Gelbart, cited in Carol Tavris's insightful book *Anger: The Misunderstood Emotion* (New York: Simon & Schuster, 1982), pp. 149–150.

2. Step to Their Side

"Rarely is it advisable": Fortune de Felice, "Negotiations or the Art of Negotiating," in I. William Zartman, ed., *The 50% Solution* (New Haven: Yale University Press, 1976), p. 56.

An AT&T sales team: This account comes from a personal conversation with an AT&T executive, autumn 1985.

"Everything has been said before": André Gide, *Le Traite du Narcisse*, 1891.

Consider a contract negotiation: This example comes from William F. Whyte's excellent case study *Pattern for Industrial Peace* (New York: Harper, 1951), pp. 87–88 and 182–183.

Former U.S. Defense Secretary Robert McNamara: This example comes from my personal notes taken at the meeting.

Take the Columbia law professor: From K. Hegland, "Why Teach Trial Advocacy?: An Essay on Never Ask Why" in "Humanistic Education," monograph III, J. Himmelstein and H. Lesnick, eds. (New York: Columbia University School of Education), p. 69.

Consider how an American diplomat: This story is cited in Dr. Julius Segal, *Winning Life's Toughest Battles: Roots of Human Resilience* (New York: Ivy Books, 1986), p. 41.

An American senator: I owe this example to Elizabeth Sherwood.

Consider the example of a fund-raiser for the United Way: For this story I am indebted to Pedro Freyre.

People also use different "sensory languages": For further information about the importance of matching the other person's sensory orientation, see the work of John Grinder and Richard Bandler, e.g., *Frogs into Princes* (Moab, Utah: Real People Press, 1979).

Make "I" statements, not "You" statements: For an excellent discussion of this point as it applies to parents and children, see Dr. Thomas Gordon, *P.E.T.: Parent Effectiveness Training* (New York: Plume, 1975), pp. 115–138.

A leading child psychologist: Haim G. Ginott, *Between Parent and Child* (New York: Avon, 1956), p. 138.

3. Reframe

In 1979, the SALT II arms-control treaty: This example comes from a conversation with Joseph R. Biden, Jr., in May 1983.

In the acquisitions negotiation: Victor Kiam, *Going for It! How to Succeed as an Entrepreneur* (New York: William Morrow, 1986), p. 178.

"We like deadlines": E. C. "Mike" Ackerman, personal communication to the author, autumn 1987.

Take the eighteenth-century general: *The Little, Brown Book of Anecdotes*, Clifton Fadiman, general ed. (Boston: Little, Brown, 1985), p. 222.

4. Build Them a Golden Bridge

A classic example is the failure: This account is drawn from Al Neuharth's memoir *Confessions of an S.O.B.* (New York: Doubleday, 1989).

"When I was about thirteen": Steven Spielberg, quoted in *Time*, July 15, 1985. I am grateful to Arthur Kanegis for bringing this example to my attention.

"I turn towards the other person": Francois Walder, *The Negotiators* (New York: McDowell, Obolensky, 1959), p. 12.

"When the conversation began": Fortune de Felice, *op. cit.*, p. 57.

Take the example of the homeowner: This story comes from Edward Lustig.

Take the acquisitions negotiator for Campbell Soup: This account comes from a personal conversation with a Campbell's executive, autumn 1983.

"They're all rational": Ackerman, *op. cit.*

Often the secret: For a good discussion of hostage negotiation techniques, see G. Dwayne Fuselier, "A practical overview of hostage negotiation," *FBI Law Enforcement Bulletin*, vol. 50, July 1981.

Consider the face-saving skill: Fadiman, *op. cit.* p. 129.

Take the avid fisherman: For this story, I am grateful to Joseph Haubenhofer.

When British Prime Minister Benjamin Disraeli: Fadiman, *op. cit.*, p. 171.

Go Slow to Go Fast: I owe this phrase to Michael Doyle and David Straus. They use it in their pathbreaking book *Making Meetings Work* (New York: Playboy Press, 1976).

He [the prison director]: Charles W. Thayer, *Diplomat* (New York: Harper, 1959), pp. 90–91.

5. Use Power to Educate

"To win one hundred victories": Sun Tzu, *The Art of War*, translated by Samuel B. Griffith (Oxford, England: Oxford University Press, 1963), p. 96.

When Chrysler Corporation: Lee Iacocca with William Novak, *Iacocca: An Autobiography* (New York: Bantam, 1984), pp. 218–19.

Take the situation of an exclusive department store: This example comes from Saul D. Alinsky, *Rules for Radicals* (New York: Vintage Books, 1972), pp. 146–47.

"The more brutal your methods": Basil Liddell Hart, *Strategy* (New York: Signet, 1974), p. 357.

At the outset of the Cuban missile crisis: For an excellent account of presidential decision-making in this crisis, see Graham T. Allison, *Essence of Decision* (Boston: Little, Brown, 1971) and Robert F. Kennedy, *Thirteen Days: A Memoir of the Cuban Missile Crisis* (New York: W. W. Norton, 1969).

"Absolute power, Templar": For this Churchill anecdote, I am grateful to Ambassador Jamsheed Marker.

In 1943 hundreds of German women: This incident is described in a doctoral study by Nathan Stoltzfus of Harvard University. For a brief description of the protest, see Nathan Stoltzfus, "The Women's Rosenstrasse Protest in Nazi Berlin," in *Nonviolent Sanctions* (Winter 1989/90), p. 3.

Consider the intervention approach: For a full discussion of the intervention technique, see Vernon E. Johnson, *Intervention* (Minneapolis: Johnson Institute Books, 1986).

Consider the tactic adopted by tenants: Alinsky, *op. cit.*, p. 144.

In the military chronicles of ancient China: Sun Tzu, *op. cit.*, p. 79.

A typical dispute resolution procedure: For a discussion of dispute resolution procedures, see William L. Ury, Jeanne M. Brett, and Stephen B. Goldberg, *Getting Disputes Resolved* (San Francisco: Jossey-Bass, 1988).

In the wake of the Cuban missile crisis: See Robert F. Kennedy, *op. cit.*, pp. 105–106.

"We save some flexibility for the end": Ackerman, *op. cit.*

Conclusion

A hostage negotiation: This account is drawn from newspaper accounts and a personal interview with retired Detective Lieutenant Robert J. Louden, on February 8, 1991.

During the American Civil War: Fadiman, *op. cit.* p. 360.

About the Author

A negotiator, public speaker, and bestselling author, William Ury directs the Global Negotiation Project at Harvard University. He is coauthor of *Getting to Yes* and author of *The Third Side* and a new book, *The Power of a Positive No: How to Say No and Still Get to Yes*. Over the past three decades, Ury has mediated in conflicts ranging from coal strikes to boardroom battles to civil wars around the world. He has taught negotiation to tens of thousands of leaders in business, government, and the nonprofit sector.

Ury is cofounder of the e-Parliament (www.e-parl.net), a problem-solving forum for effective legislation, connecting members of Congress and Parliament around the world. He also leads the Abraham Path Initiative (www.abrahampath.org), which seeks to create a permanent path of tourism and pilgrimage in the Middle East that retraces the footsteps of Abraham, the unifying figure of Judaism, Christianity, and Islam.

Trained as an anthropologist, Ury holds a B.A. from Yale and a Ph.D. from Harvard.

For further information, please visit www.williamury.com or send an e-mail to info@williamury.com.